# Vocabulary in Action

## Lessons from
## Great Literacy Teachers

Gay Fawcett

ROWMAN & LITTLEFIELD EDUCATION

A division of
ROWMAN & LITTLEFIELD PUBLISHERS, INC.
*Lanham • New York • Toronto • Plymouth, UK*

KH

Published in the United States of America
Published by Rowman & Littlefield Education
A division of Rowman & Littlefield Publishers, Inc.
A wholly owned subsidary of The Rowman & Littlefield Publishing Group, Inc.
4501 Forbes Boulevard, Suite 200, Lanham, Maryland 20706
www.rowman.com

10 Thornbury Road, Plymouth PL6 7PP, United Kingdom

British Library Cataloguing in Publication Information Available

**Library of Congress Cataloging-in-Publication Data**

Fawcett, Gay.
  Vocabulary in action : lessons from great literacy teachers / Gay Fawcett.
     p. cm.
  ISBN 978-1-61048-875-4 (cloth : alk. paper) — ISBN 978-1-61048-876-1
(pbk. : alk. paper) — ISBN 978-1-61048-877-8 (electronic)
  1.  Vocabulary—Study and teaching (Elementary)—United States. 2.
Language arts (Elementary)—United States.  I. Title.
  LB1574.5.F38 2012
  372.44—dc23

                                                        2012022261

∞™ The paper used in this publication meets the minimum requirements of American
National Standard for Information Sciences—Permanence of Paper for Printed Library
Materials, ANSI/NISO Z39.48-1992.

Printed in the United States of America

11/12/13

"The stuff that comes with the child is not science, logic, or mechanical skill. It is soul stuff. It is imagination, heart, and creativity. It is spirit and vision."

—*Education and the Soul* by John P. Miller

Dedicated to Elijah and Lily who continually renew my soul

# Contents

# Foreword

## Timothy V. Rasinski

Knowing a word means more than simply "sounding it out." Phonics or word recognition instruction is clearly important—people cannot read if they cannot decode the words they find in print. Yet phonics is not enough. Good readers need to understand the meanings of the words they encounter in print—this is vocabulary. Although much of a person's vocabulary is developed through normal speech interactions, such interactions are not sufficient to develop one's vocabulary for reading. Authors embed in their texts literary words that are not often used in daily oral speech (good writing is often measured by the words that an author uses). If readers are not familiar with the meanings of these words, their understanding of the texts they read will be limited. Similarly, informational texts often contain specialized academic vocabulary that is essential for text comprehension.

Although it makes good sense that vocabulary instruction is an important part of any effective reading curriculum, it seems that vocabulary is still taught in the traditional rote memorization manner. Students are presented with a list of words to look up in a dictionary and are expected to memorize each definition for a test at the end of the week—and end up forgetting the words a few days after being tested. No wonder many students struggle with vocabulary! No wonder students come to hate word study!

In recent years, many effective instructional strategies have been developed for teaching vocabulary to students, and many textbooks on reading instruction present these strategies to teachers. What is missing from these textbook presentations are the stories of real teachers who have made vocabulary instruction a priority in their classrooms. *Vocabulary in Action* fills this gap. Gay Fawcett has collected the actual stories of teachers who have adapted the strategies that have been identified through research and scholarship to their own style of teaching and the needs of their students. In this book, for example, you will read how a teacher from Virginia explores Latin and Greek word roots with her elementary students to discover the meanings of English words and how another teacher from Maryland helps students use context to unlock the meaning of words found in the texts they read. These stories are presented not as prescriptions on how to teach vocabulary but as examples of how creative and knowledgeable teachers can make vocabulary instruction effective and engaging for students.

Great teaching is both a science and an art. The science of teaching vocabulary is well established. We know that vocabulary knowledge is important for reading comprehension; we know that certain words (academic and literary words in particular) are essential for readers' understanding; and we know effective instructional approaches have been developed for helping students expand and deepen their vocabularies. The art of teaching vocabulary emerges when individual teachers employ and adapt the scientific knowledge of vocabulary instruction in their own special ways that are creative and engaging and that boost students' knowledge of words. *Vocabulary in Action* will give you, the reader, an insider's look at how great teachers transform science into art in their classrooms. Hopefully their stories will inspire you to make vocabulary instruction both an art and science in your own classroom and school.

# Preface

Recently Mark, a kindergarten teacher, told me about his typical first day of school. Some students get off the bus never having registered for school. "What's your name?" Mark asks. They often reply with some variation of "Sissy" or "Bubba." Mark persists, "What's your last name?" Sissy and Bubba stare blankly. "Where do you live?" Bubba smiles, "With Mommy."

The expression in Mark's voice says he's never gotten used to the fact that some of his students don't know the meaning of common words like *crash*, *storm*, or *plant*. "If they don't know their own names," he sighs, "why do I expect them to know common vocabulary?" Do these children struggle with learning to read? Mark nods his head and says simply, "Yes."

Extensive research has confirmed what Mark knows firsthand: there is a strong connection between vocabulary and reading achievement (Beck, McKeown, & Kucan, 2002; National Reading Panel, 2000; Stahl, 1998). As you will see in chapter 1, limited word knowledge is especially prevalent among children from low-income families. However, a vocabulary gap is not limited to such populations.

Like Mark, I learned firsthand the impact of limited vocabulary on reading success. Unlike Mark, I taught in an upper-middle-class town with two major universities nearby. David was the oldest of five children from a well-to-do family. David had a speech impediment and lacked the common vocabulary of most children in my class. After trying several interventions with little success, I referred David to the school psychologist. He did not qualify for special education services, although he did qualify for speech and language services. He continued to struggle with reading and finished first grade nearly a full year behind most of his classmates.

David's brother Matthew was next. Then Christie, Thomas, and Joshua. Each had difficulty learning to read. By the time Christie began school, however, teachers who taught these children had uncovered some telling information. The children's father owned a company, and his wife worked for him. One parent was always there when the children got home from school, but both parents continued to work late into the evening, so TV became the babysitter. The children heard plenty of language, but acquiring a rich vocabulary requires more than hearing words; it requires interaction with words. Children must use words multiple times and in multiple contexts before they can own them.

Many children start school already behind because of a limited vocabulary, and the problem cuts across socioeconomic status. Children from low-income homes frequently lack the types of social interaction that lead to a strong vocabulary. At the same time, the hectic work and social schedules of some of today's middle-class and affluent families leave children like David and his siblings lacking adult attention that immerses them in rich language.

In addition, the "plugged in" generation often substitutes technology for human dialogue. A recent study found that 35 percent of children ages six months to three years have a TV in their bedroom, and 10 percent of children ages four to eight have a computer in their bedroom (Rosen, 2010). Moreover, in a recent TV newscast, Dr. Margaret Richards, physician at the Cleveland Clinic, expressed concern that more and more parents are seen texting when they should be interacting with their children in places like parks, zoos, restaurants, and stores (Vecchio, 2010).

Although at face value the situation may seem dire, research has repeatedly shown that great literacy teachers can positively influence vocabulary acquisition (Baumann, Kame'enui, & Ask, 2003; Blachowicz & Fisher, 2000; National Reading Panel, 2000). Quality instruction makes a difference! You make a difference! Hopefully this book will be a valuable resource as you help students acquire rich vocabularies that will serve them in their schoolwork, in their relationships, and in their lives.

# Acknowledgments

Someone has always believed in me as a writer, and so here I am—my first book in hand.

I was a little child filling a red notebook with stories of "Hankie and the Hawk," "The Weiner and the Hot Dog," "The Clown," and "The Little Angel." My mother didn't know about the writing process, the difference between active and passive voice, or where to put a semicolon; but my mother knew she had a little girl who thrived on encouragement, so she told me how wonderful my stories were, and I kept writing.

I was a third grader slipping a story on my teacher's desk when she wasn't looking. Mrs. DeHoff knew the shy little girl didn't want attention, so she quietly knelt down beside my desk and whispered something wonderful into my ear, and I kept writing.

I was a doctoral student taking the course *Teaching Writing as a Process*. Dr. McCracken didn't know that the writer in me had sat dormant for so long, but because of one encouraging remark, "You should submit this piece somewhere for publication," I became a published author, and I kept writing.

I was an educator with a Ph.D. writing articles for professional journals when my doctoral advisors, Dr. Nancy Padak and Dr. Tim Rasinski, began asking me to coauthor books with them. To see my name alongside theirs on the covers of books has been one of the greatest accomplishments of my career, and I keep writing.

I was an author desiring a book of my own when Tom Koerner, vice president and editorial director of Rowman & Littlefield, saw the potential in my proposal, and so I wrote this book.

It would have never happened without the talented teachers who shared ideas, welcomed me into their classrooms, and showered me with patience as I asked question after question to be sure I was getting their stories just right.

These dedicated teachers nurture the imagination, heart, and creativity in their students every day: Susan Dowell, Patrick Hernan, Abby Lowe, Sally Maher, Joanna Newton, Michele McCombs, Jill Johnson-McMullen, Stephanie Murphy, Jeri Powers, Elaina Vann, and Jackie Zaucha. Thank you for sharing your teaching and students with the readers of this book!

Note: Special thanks to Carlie Wall, assistant editor at Rowman & Littlefield, for her assistance in preparing this manuscript. Carlie always answered my inquiries promptly and expertly guided me through the paperwork trail of publishing.

# Introduction

This book is designed to help you examine your vocabulary instruction and consider what you can do to help students who have vocabulary gaps and further enrich the vocabulary of those students who don't. Chapter 1 presents research-based background on vocabulary development and its relationship to reading achievement. In chapter 1 you will also find general guidelines for vocabulary instruction.

In chapters 2–12 you will meet great literacy teachers from around the United States who have designed successful vocabulary instruction for their grades K–6 classrooms. You will also meet some of their students, but please note that all students' names are pseudonyms.

Each chapter begins with a brief description of an essential component of effective vocabulary instruction. Each teacher will share vocabulary routines that he or she uses on a regular basis, including his or her favorite. You will find some of the vocabulary routines to be similar; however, since each teacher puts her or his own unique spin on the more common of routines, you will be able to consider how you might incorporate some of the ideas into your instruction. Many of the strategies are accompanied by student-generated examples or reproducibles that you can use as they are or adapt for your own context.

There is little evidence to support one vocabulary strategy over another. You know your students' strengths and needs better than anyone else, and you are the one who should decide whether a "best practice" is best for your students. Try out some of the strategies, evaluate how they work, and use your professional judgment and experience to adopt them, adapt them, or dump them.

Each chapter concludes with reflective questions you can use alone or with colleagues to plan the actions you will take to improve vocabulary instruction. Some chapters include professional development meeting procedures for discussing key questions. (You can also adapt these procedures to other staff development sessions or staff meetings.) Chapter 13 provides a list of print and online resources to support your vocabulary instruction.

The teachers profiled in this book were nominated by literacy experts, professors, principals, and other great literacy teachers. They were then interviewed; some were observed in their classrooms. The following criteria helped to narrow the list of nominees down to the very best:

- Vocabulary instruction is evidence based,
- Vocabulary instruction is one part of a comprehensive literacy program,
- Vocabulary is taught in meaningful contexts,
- Vocabulary instruction is followed by application in authentic contexts,
- Vocabulary words selected are useful in students' reading, writing, and conversations,
- Vocabulary instruction is systematic and in depth,
- Vocabulary instruction is both direct and indirect,
- The teacher is a lover of language and words herself or himself, and
- The teacher is a learner.

Helping students learn to read is serious business, but when you find something that works, it becomes a joyful celebration. Great vocabulary instruction works. Besides, learning new words, using new vocabulary, and playing with language are just good fun. Enjoy!

*Chapter One*

# Principles of Vocabulary Instruction

A few years ago Richard Allington wrote a poignant article entitled "If They Don't Read Much, How They Ever Gonna Get Good?" (Allington, 1977). The title speaks for itself. Few, if any, teachers would argue with Allington's premise that students become better readers if they read a lot. However, those same teachers might preface Allington's question with a question of their own: If they don't know the words, how they ever gonna read?

Vocabulary is at the heart of reading. Indeed, research over several decades has shown that an extensive oral vocabulary (expressive vocabulary) is positively linked to reading achievement in general, reading comprehension in particular, and greater academic success as a whole (Beck, McKeown, & Kucan, 2002; Curtis & Longo, 2001; National Reading Panel, 2000).

Correlations between standardized measures of vocabulary and reading comprehension are especially high—typically in the .90 or higher range regardless of the measures used or the populations tested (Stahl, 2003a). But you don't need research to convince you of that, do you? You see it every day as you work with students. If a child can't read the words she is not going to understand what she is reading; or if she can read the words but doesn't know what many of them mean, she is not going to comprehend what she is reading.

However, the research on vocabulary and reading has also revealed some interesting facts that may not be so obvious. Consider this:

- An average first grader knows between 3,000 and 6,000 words when the school year begins, and he will learn between 2,000 and 3,000 new words every year (Nagy, 1988).
- Because vocabulary constitutes a major component of IQ tests, children with limited vocabularies are often categorized as learning disabled when they really aren't (McKenna & Stahl, 2003).

1

- By fifth grade, students encounter 10,000 unknown words in their reading alone (Nagy & Anderson, 1984).
- It takes between eight and fifteen repetitions before new information is mastered (i.e., new words) (Allen, 1999; "How Many" 2010).
- The "fourth-grade slump" may be due to the increased vocabulary demand of content materials (Chall & Jacobs, 2003).

When you consider this information along with the fact that many students begin school with a vocabulary deficit, vocabulary instruction may seem to be a daunting task. However, there are routines and strategies that have proven successful in classrooms all over the country, and you will read about them in the remaining chapters of this book. First, however, we'll examine what it means to "know a word" and then discuss general guidelines for both direct and indirect vocabulary instruction.

## WHEN DOES A STUDENT *KNOW* A WORD?

There is no precise answer to the question: What does it mean to *know* a word? Word understanding falls along a continuum and is determined by the depth of knowledge a student has about the word. Stahl (2003b) explains it this way:

> Ordinarily, when we encounter a word we don't know, we skip it, especially if the word is not needed to make sense of what we are reading. But we remember something about the words that we skip. This something could be where we saw it, something about the context where it appeared, or some other aspect. This information is in memory, but the memory is not strong enough to be accessible to our conscious mind. As we encounter a word repeatedly, more and more information accumulates about that word until we have a vague notion of what it "means." As we get more information, we are able to define that word. (p. 18)

As early as 1965, Dale talked about four levels of knowing a word: (1) I never saw it before. (2) I've heard of it, but I don't know what it means. (3) I recognize it in context—it has something to do with . . . (4) I know it well. This explanation of "knowing a word" has since become an instructional strategy, sometimes known as a knowledge rating chart or vocabulary survey, where teachers ask students to rate their understanding of words before and after instruction. (p. 13)

Understanding a word depends on the multitude of ways a student can interact with the word. Can he define it? Recognize situations where the word can be used appropriately? Recognize times when the word is used inappropriately? Different ways of knowing a word require multiple encounters with the word in multiple contexts. In one research study, McKeown and her team (1985) found that four encounters with a word did not reliably improve reading comprehension, but twelve encounters did.

Earlier we noted that students learn between 2,000 and 3,000 new words per year. Divide that by the number of days they are in school and you come up with about fifteen to eighteen new words per day. How can you possibly help students attain a deep understanding of so many words?

The National Reading Panel (2000) reviewed fifty research studies spanning twenty-one years and concluded that vocabulary is learned both directly and indirectly. Direct instruction of vocabulary is essential, and most of this book is devoted to it, yet research indicates students can only learn about eight to ten new words each week through direct instruction (Stahl & Fairbanks, 1986). So before we look at direct instruction, let's consider three ways students can gain some of those new words indirectly.

## INDIRECT LEARNING OF VOCABULARY

### Read Alouds

In this age of high-stakes testing, classroom read alouds sometimes take a backseat to skills instruction and test prep; however, since a young child's listening vocabulary (receptive vocabulary) is about two years ahead of her reading vocabulary (Bicmiller, 2001), hearing stories read aloud is a good test prep investment in its own right.

Isabel Beck, a leading researcher in the area of vocabulary, uses the term *robust vocabulary* when she talks about what can result from read alouds (Beck, McKeown, & Kucan, 2002). Beck and her colleagues suggest that early reading materials are not good sources for adding new words to young children's vocabulary repertoires because the materials frequently are written with controlled vocabulary. With so many children's quality informational texts available today, it's easy to integrate read alouds into your classroom routine, not just as an after-recess calming activity but throughout the day as you teach science, social studies, and math.

Although reading aloud may be a way to teach vocabulary *indirectly*, it should not be happenstance. Research shows that effective teachers intentionally plan for discussing new words encountered in read alouds. Look for children's authors who use wonderful vocabulary. Some of my favorites are William Steig, Bill Peet, and Patricia Polacco. Notice the robust

4

language in this excerpt from William Steig's (2011) book, *The Amazing Bone*:

> The bone commenced to revile the fox. "You coward," it sneered. "You worm, you odoriferous wretch!" These expletives were annoying. "Shut up, or I'll eat you," the fox snarled.

Recently I read this story to my grandchildren. I asked four-year-old Lily what she thought *snarled* means. She replied, "He said it mean." Seven-year-old Elijah deduced that *wretch* means, "Kind of like a blockhead or a dummy." (He got that "blockhead" vocabulary from reading too many Peanuts comics!)

According to Stahl's (2003b) explanation of what it means to know a word, the information about those words is now in Lily's and Elijah's memories at some level, but the memories are probably not strong enough to be accessible to their conscious minds. As they encounter those words repeatedly, more and more information will accumulate about the words until they have added the words to their speaking, and subsequently reading, vocabularies.

The more actively and deeply the child processes a new word, the more likely he will recognize and use it in other contexts. I was reading *The Hundred Dresses* (Estes, 1994) to my third graders when I came upon the sentence, "They still felt disconsolate, and Maddie wondered if she were going to be unhappy about Wanda and the hundred dresses forever."

I felt fairly certain my students did not know the meaning of *disconsolate*, but I kept reading. At the end of the chapter I said, "Let's go back and listen to this sentence again." I read the sentence and then asked what they thought *disconsolate* might mean. Stephen replied, "I think it means they are sad." When asked for reasons, Stephen replied that the story said the girls felt bad about what they had done, and Maddie could not get to sleep that night.

Though Stephen did not have a precise definition of the word *disconsolate*, he certainly had a good initial understanding. Would Stephen (and the other children) remember the word later? Probably not, so I looked for opportunities to use the word in our everyday classroom conversations. "Shelly, you seem disconsolate today. What's wrong?" or "Our kitten died, and my whole family is feeling disconsolate."

Of course robust vocabulary is not just for book discussions. We dare not overlook the importance of conversations with children as another way of building a strong vocabulary.

## Talk with Children

In a large study of family language use, Hart and Risley (2003) found that by age four children of professional families heard 45 million words, whereas children of mothers who were on welfare heard only 13 million words, thus creating a "30 million word gap." The results of a follow-up study were not surprising; the "30 million word gap" was a strong predictor of third-grade reading comprehension.

However, as pointed out in the preface to this book, low vocabulary acquisition is not solely a problem in lower socioeconomic families. Most U.S. parents converse with their children for only about thirty-eight minutes per week (Hansen, 2010). Even children from middle- and upper-class families sometimes lack the social interaction necessary to build a solid vocabulary base.

Morrow and Tracey (2007) suggest a "reciprocal relationship" between children's spoken and written language. In other words, each helps develop the other. The more they understand spoken words, the more words they can read. The more words they can read, the more spoken words they understand. Classroom talk is imperative for this reciprocal relationship. Children must be involved in frequent and substantive conversations. Often, however, classroom talk becomes lost in a cycle more like interrogation than discussion, as illustrated in figure 1.1.

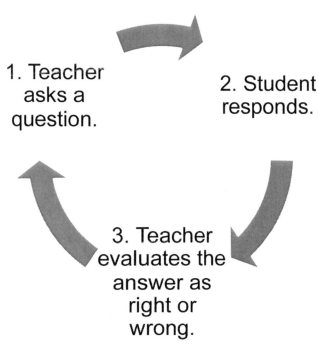

**1. Teacher asks a question.**

**2. Student responds.**

**3. Teacher evaluates the answer as right or wrong.**

**Figure 1.1.   Discussion Cycle**

Mary Budd Rowe was a pioneer in studying classroom talk. She gathered data in over eight hundred classrooms. Some of her surprising findings are shown in figure 1.2 (Rowe, 1972).

Rowe (1972) began another study to find out what would happen if teachers waited three seconds instead of one second before responding to students' answers and found that classroom talk improved dramatically.

- Among high achievers, the increase in length of explanations was about 500 percent. Among children who struggle in school, the increase was about 700 percent.
- The number of unsolicited but appropriate comments increased.
- As high as 30 percent of students in some classrooms had not participated in classroom talk before. With a three-second wait time, failures to respond dropped to less than 5 percent.
- The number of questions asked by children increased.
- Disciplinary problems decreased.

Rowe also observed positive changes in teacher behaviors.

- Their questioning strategies tended to be more varied and flexible.
- They decreased the quantity and increased the quality and variety of their questions.

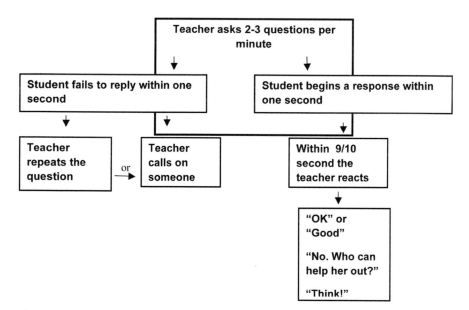

**Figure 1.2.  Classroom Talk**

• They asked additional questions that required more complex information processing and higher-level thinking on the part of students.

Although Rowe's initial research is decades old, a visit to many classrooms today will show that there is more reality than cliché to the saying "We teach as we were taught." Even though some of your students may come to school with language deficits, you can make a difference by restructuring the way talk takes place in your classroom—one second versus three seconds can make a huge difference!

In addition to providing more wait time, an important component of quality discussions is the level of vocabulary you use with your students. Children love big words. Use words you would not normally use with your students and watch what happens. Young children have a natural curiosity about new words, so we don't need to "talk down" to them. Through ongoing conversations they begin to build a speaking vocabulary that will provide the foundation for reading vocabulary.

## Independent Reading

There is a strong association between students' progress in reading and the amount of authentic reading they do (Block & Mangieri, 2002; Krashen, 2001, 2004; Stanovich, 1986). Yet the unfortunate truth is most students read little either in or out of school. The Scholastic 2008 Kids and Family Reading Report, a follow-up to a similar 2006 study, found only one in four children ages five to seventeen say they read books for fun every day.

In terms of vocabulary acquisition, by the end of second grade, students who read at least twenty minutes a day have been exposed to 4.5 million more words than students who read just five minutes a day, and almost 5.4 million more words than students who read just one minute a day. The numbers grow exponentially as students progress through the grades (Reading Research, 2009–2010).

As with the fate of read alouds, today's test prep frenzy often replaces the time students once had for programs like sustained silent reading (SSR) and drop everything and read (DEAR). Some teachers rationalize dropping independent reading time with the argument that many students don't actually read during SSR anyway. However, several studies have shown that about 90 percent of students do read if provided time to do so in school (Cohen, 1999; Herda & Ramos, 2001; Von Sprecken & Krashen, 1998). Exposing students to thousands of vocabulary words through independent reading is an excellent preparation for reading test materials.

Beware! sustained silent reading may not always be silent. Sometimes students should read in pairs or small groups, and there will be noise. Younger students may need to subvocalize, so you can teach them to "whisper read."

One of the best SSR pictures I carry in my head is from one of my first-grade classes. Students were reading quietly, when I detected a little giggle, then another, and another. Kristen had discovered *Cloudy with a Chance of Meatballs* (Barrett & Barrett, 1978). Soon a child beside her leaned over, and Kristen began reading aloud. Another child joined, then another, and another until the entire class—except Jeremy—was enjoying Kristen's book with her. Jeremy was so absorbed in his own book that he never even knew what he had missed.

Don't forget the message you send when you also read during independent reading time. As tempting as it might be to grade that stack of papers or have a reading conference with a student, children need to see an adult they respect laughing over a funny magazine article, crying over a sad book, or frowning over that complicated research report you've been trying to get through.

The sharing that takes place after independent reading is just as important as the reading itself. Once again, it's an opportunity for students to use the vocabulary that is somewhere on their word knowledge continuum. Of course you won't have time for all students to share every day, but you can have a few students share what they read and let the others share with partners or in small groups. Be sure to share what you've read sometimes. This would be a good time to model the enjoyment of different genres. Independent reading is an important component of vocabulary acquisition so be sure to share that information with parents.

## DIRECT VOCABULARY INSTRUCTION

The remaining chapters will be devoted to direct vocabulary instruction. Following are some general principles to keep in mind as you read about specific procedures and strategies great literacy teachers use.

### What Works?

In its review of vocabulary research, the National Reading Panel (2000, pp. 4–24) found the following strategies to be effective:

• Keyword method: Children learn new words by associating a keyword with the new vocabulary word. A keyword is a word that sounds like the new word and is easily pictured. In our earlier example, if I wanted to help Elijah associate the word *wretch* with a keyword, I might have him think of the word *fetch* and mentally picture a dog carrying someone who is ragged, tired, and helpless.

- Incidental learning: Most vocabulary is learned through reading, listening to others read, and actively participating in conversations.
- Repeated exposure: Using new vocabulary across the curriculum increases school achievement.
- Rich contexts: Activities that extend the use of learned words beyond the classroom result in deeper learning of the words.
- Preteaching of vocabulary increases both vocabulary and comprehension.
- Restructuring reading materials, such as using an easier synonym to explain a harder word, yields significant vocabulary gains.
- Context clues: Children use clues in the text to help decipher new words.

## What Words?

With these findings in mind, then, how do you decide which words to teach? Beck, McKeown, and Kucan (2002) suggest you consider vocabulary needs on three levels:

- Sight words/high-frequency words, which do not require a great amount of teaching,
- Vocabulary words that occur in a wide variety of texts, the common words children use in everyday conversations and encounter often in reading,
- Words frequently used in content areas, which are words not often used in everyday language but needed for subject matter learning.

## Guidelines for Vocabulary Instruction

1. Select words that children will encounter in reading or conversations.

     I was visiting a sixth-grade classroom one Friday afternoon. Vocabulary instruction was of the traditional variety:

     Monday—Students given a list of ten words

     Tuesday—Look up the words in a dictionary and write the definitions

     Wednesday—Use each word in a sentence

     Thursday—Write each word five times in order to learn the spelling

     Friday—Vocabulary test (usually matching or fill in the blank)

     One word on the week's list was *celibacy*. After class, curious as to where the words came from, I asked the teacher about that word in particular. "Oh," she replied, "it's just on there in case someday they need to know it." While it's sometimes difficult to know what words children will need, usually common sense will help you sort through those that are probably not a good investment for your limited instructional time.

2. Teach words that are necessary for understanding the text.

Students should learn early on the self-monitoring strategy, *skip it and read on*, to decide if they need an unknown word for understanding. Have you ever observed a student who spent so much time trying to read a character's name that he totally lost what the story was about? One day when my third-grade class was having after-SSR sharing, I told them about the book I was reading, *Crime and Punishment* (Dostoyevsky, 1989). I said,

> This book is written by a Russian author named Dostoyevsky. Because he's Russian he used Russian names in the book, and they are all very long. I could take the time to sound them out, but I don't really care about their names. What I care about is what's happening in the story, so I call them Miss B and Mr. R and I go on with the story. You can do that, too. When you come to a name and you don't need it to understand the story, call them Betty or Joe and go on.

Our principal, Ms. Schofield, regularly invited groups of students to her office to read to her. The group chosen to go shortly after my mini-lesson picked a Japanese folktale to read. Later Ms. Schofield shared what had happened. When Jason, a struggling reader, came upon the Japanese character's name, Naroshimo Taro, he paused. Nicole said softly, "Call him Joe." Every student who followed Jason in reading also called the character *Joe*. When they finished the story Ms. Schofield asked why they had done that, and Nicole responded, "We wanted you to understand the story, but you don't need that hard name to do that."

When we teach students to use reading strategies, we also must teach them when and how to use them, so a few days later I purposefully planned a lesson that would lead to a discussion of when one cannot skip names. I read the traditional folktale *Tikki Tikki Tembo* (Mosel, 2007). Of course if we skipped the character's name in that story (Tikki tikki tembo-no sa rembo-chari bari ruchi pip peri pembo) there would be no plot. Then we had a discussion about other times when it would be important to know a name (in social studies or science, for example).

3. Teach high-frequency words.

Students need to learn sight words such as those on the Dolch or Fry lists. However, as Rasinski reminds us in *The Fluent Reader* (2003), "One potential drawback to reading words in isolation is that it may reinforce the notion that reading is simply about identifying individual words. This could lead to word-by-word reading in some children" (p. 94). Teach high-frequency words in context. A good place to start is by putting sight words into meaningful phrases.

4. Teach interesting words.

   The best way to choose interesting words is to become a word lover yourself. Be alert to interesting words in daily conversations, on the TV or radio, and in things you read. Share them with students. Students will learn that words are fun when you use vocabulary like *spiffy*, *scruffy*, *truffle*, *onomatopoeia*, *bioluminescence*, and *scuffle*.

5. Teach vocabulary-building words.

   Learning Latin and Greek roots (prefixes, suffixes, and base words) allows students to break words into meaningful parts so that they can determine definitions. For example, by knowing that *bi* means "two," students can deduce the meanings of words such as *bicycle*, *biannual*, *bicentennial*, and *biaxial*. (See chapter 3 for more on teaching with Greek and Latin roots.)

6. Teach words in relation to other words.

   The human brain learns by making connections. Help students see the relationship between *nation* and *nationality*; *transportation* and *transport*; *compassion*, *passion*, and *compassionate*; *hospital* and *hospice*; *disconsolate* and *console*; *argue*, *argument*, *argumentative*; and so on.

7. Teach students to relate words to their schema.

   Put words into contexts that are familiar by using metaphors, similes, and analogies. For example, to teach the word *obstinate*, you might use the following simile: Mary is as obstinate as a mule.

8. Teach words systematically and in depth.

   Have a specific plan that includes read alouds, independent reading, conversations, and direct vocabulary instruction. Ask students to *do* something with the words beyond looking them up in the dictionary and using them in sentences. Have them restate the meaning in their own words, use them in conversation, or use them in their writing.

## CONCLUSION

There is an abundance of research showing that students whose parents are involved do better in school. However, the reality is there are many parents whom we do not engage, for numerous reasons, despite our best efforts. Thankfully the research is also clear that great teachers can help to overcome that obstacle.

Marzano's research found students of teachers characterized as "most effective" posted achievement gains of 53 percentage points. In classrooms led by "least effective" teachers, student achievement gains averaged 14 percentage points (Marzano, 2004).

Doug Reeves has published a number of articles on what have become known as the 90-90-90 schools. Reeves examined schools where 90 percent or more of the students were eligible for free and reduced cost meals, 90 percent or more of the students were members of ethnic minority groups, and 90 percent or more of the students met the district or state academic standards in reading or another area (Reeves, 2000). Reeves pointed to the classroom teacher as the variable that made the difference in those schools.

I could cite many more teacher effectiveness studies, but you don't need research to tell you about the difference a teacher can make, do you? You see it every day as you work with students.

In the chapters that follow, some great literacy teachers who are making a difference will share their vocabulary instruction with you. Of course no single instructional method will result in optimal learning for every student, so take what will work for your teaching style, your students, and your school context. Great vocabulary instruction depends on you, the teacher who knows her students' learning needs better than anyone else.


## REFLECTION AND ACTION

The following questions are designed to help you think through your vocabulary instruction, either alone or with a group of colleagues. The reflection you do is an important part of reading the chapter. The action that results is what puts you among the ranks of "great literacy teachers."

1. What was the most important thing you learned in this chapter? Why?
2. In order to be an effective vocabulary teacher, you have to be a word lover yourself. The following websites provide a new word every day. Learn three new words this week and use them in various contexts until you feel you know the words at a deep level.
   A.Word.A.Day: http://www.wordsmith.org/awad/
   Merriam Webster Word of the Day: http://www.merriam-webster.com/cgi-bin/mwwod.pl
   Dictionary.com: http://dictionary.reference.com/wordoftheday/
   Word Think: http://www.wordthink.com/
3. Analyze your wait time (audio- or videotaping will help you gather the information without distracting you from teaching). What did you observe about yourself? Make some changes and analyze your wait time again. What did you observe about your students?
4. Consider the 30 million-word gap study alongside the 90-90-90 studies. What conclusions can you draw? What are the implications for your vocabulary instruction?

5. Find three children's books that are new to you and that use robust vocabulary. What kinds of conversations could you have with your students about these books?
6. Consider the vocabulary requirements of your curriculum. Make a list of words for each of Beck, McKeown, and Kucan's (2002) levels:
   • Sight words/high-frequency words, which do not require a great amount of teaching,
   • Vocabulary words that occur in a wide variety of texts, the common words children use in everyday conversations and encounter often in reading,
   • Words frequently used in content areas.
7. What is one thing from this chapter that you would like to include in your own classroom?

## KNOWLEDGE RATING CHART

A knowledge rating chart provides the teacher with diagnostic information to guide instruction. This activity also helps students come to understand that knowing the meaning of a word is not something that happens all at once.

1. Provide students with a list of vocabulary words prior to the lesson, story, or unit.
2. Students mark each word:
   – I never saw it before.
   • I've heard of it, but I don't know what it means.
   ✓ I recognize it in context—it has something to do with . . .
   + I know it well.
3. You can have a class discussion of what they know, don't know, or students have misconceptions about. You can also use it as a pretest to guide your instruction.
4. Check the same list after the lesson, story, or unit of study. Discuss.

Title or Topic
   – I never saw it before.
   • I've heard of it, but I don't know what it means.
   ✓ I recognize it in context—it has something to do with . . .
   + I know it well.

| Before Learning | After Learning |
| --- | --- |
| 1. _____ | 1. _____ |
| 2. _____ | 2. _____ |
| 3. _____ | 3. _____ |
| 4. _____ | 4. _____ |

# Chapter Two

# The Importance of Routines
# in Vocabulary Instruction

Students need and want routines. If you doubt that, ask any substitute teacher or any teacher who has had a substitute in his or her classroom. It's not unusual for students to waste time, act out, or lose focus when their daily routine is interrupted. Routines save teachers' valuable time since planning new activities is minimized. More importantly, routines save students' valuable learning time since teachers don't have to provide instruction once the routine is initially learned. In addition, students become independent learners because they do not have to rely on the teacher for directions on what to do next.

The teachers in this book will share numerous vocabulary strategies, and there's no doubt that variety generates student interest; however, vocabulary instruction also needs to include a measure of predictability with routines that occur at regular times in your language arts instruction. In addition to the variety of strategies they will share, every teacher in this book will talk about vocabulary activities they do on a regular basis because they have learned firsthand the importance of routines in the classroom.

## VOCABULARY ROUTINE IN PARCHMENT, MICHIGAN

Routines make any classroom run more smoothly, but while the diversity in a classroom is great, the independence students develop as a result of routines is especially significant. Stephanie Murphy knows that as well as any teacher. Stephanie teaches a multiage class of third and fourth graders at Northwood Elementary School in Parchment, Michigan. The two grades are separated for language arts instruction, with Stephanie teaching language arts and another teacher handling math and science. When both grades are taken into account, it's not unusual for Stephanie to teach students reading on first-grade level, students reading on fifth-grade level, and students on every level in between. To add to the diversity, over 50 percent of students in the school receive free and reduced cost meals, yet many of the students come from highly educated middle-class homes. Stephanie's weekly vocabulary routine simultaneously develops independence and brings students together through partner work.

## Selecting Vocabulary Words

Stephanie explained why she developed her vocabulary routine. "My district uses an adopted basal program. No commercial program can meet the needs of all my students, so my routine is designed to enhance that reading program." Stephanie feels her teacher's manual presents too many new vocabulary words for each story. Her goal is to narrow down the list so that students learn a few words well rather than simply touching on many words at a surface level.

Stephanie uses a process called "check and double-check," which she learned in a professional development session, to narrow down the vocabulary list for each story. (See chapter 10 for more on professional development and vocabulary instruction.)

1. First Stephanie eliminates words that the majority of third and fourth graders should know. For example, a recent basal vocabulary list included the words *fund-raiser*, *rhythm*, and *beam*. Stephanie determined that most of her students would have encountered those words in school projects, music class, and physical education class.
2. Next Stephanie looks for words she's "nearly 100 percent positive" students will not know. Some recent examples included *blaring*, *murmur*, and *debut*.
3. Then Stephanie double-checks to see if students know those words. Sometimes she initiates a class discussion to double-check students' understanding of the words she has targeted. At other times she asks students to turn to a partner and define the words. After a recent partner-share, students reported back that few partners knew the words *blaring*, *murmur*, and *debut*.
4. Next Stephanie eliminates words that students will rarely encounter in their reading or in conversations. For example, a story the students recently read contained a number of musical terms. Stephanie explained the words as the students encountered them in the text, but she did not focus on those words in her vocabulary instruction because the likelihood of third and fourth graders needing the musical terms for future reading or writing was slim.

5. Finally, from the words that remain Stephanie selects those that students will need most because they will likely be encountered in reading and conversations in the future.

At this point, the list has gone from around fifteen words to three to five words. This shorter list becomes the focus for Stephanie's five-day vocabulary instruction routine.

## Five-Day Plan

Day 1: Stephanie begins direct vocabulary instruction by going through the list one word at a time. She reads each word to the students and then asks the class to read the words together, after which she provides her own definitions. When she taught the word *gasp*, for example, she told students, "*Gasp* is when you catch your breath quickly." When she finds it hard to put her definition into student-friendly terms, she consults an online student dictionary such as http://www.wordcentral.com/.

After the word has been defined, Stephanie provides an example as well as a nonexample of the word. For *gasped* she told the students, "If someone jumped out and scared you, you might *gasp*." For a nonexample she said, "Right now you are just sitting on the floor and breathing normally. There is no reason for you to *gasp*." Sometimes nonexamples are inherent in the list. When teaching the words *murmur* and *blaring*, for example, Stephanie demonstrated the difference between a *blaring* radio and a *murmuring* voice.

Finally on this day, students are paired with a partner to review all the words and their definitions. Pairs are given two words, and each partner provides the definition, an example, and a nonexample for their word.

Day 2: On the second day students apply their understanding of the vocabulary words by creating mental organizers (see figure 2.1). Stephanie sees the organizers as a great strategy for classrooms where there is a wide range in student ability. She honors their learning styles by allowing students to write or draw on their organizers. For example, for the word *glowered* Nate drew a picture of a mean face as an example and a smiling face as a nonexample. Owen, on the other hand, requested, "Can I write down something?" Some students choose to use both words and illustrations to fill in their organizers.

Students add the organizers to their vocabulary notebooks so that they have a ready reference when they need to revisit a word. Stephanie uses the notebooks to review vocabulary words on a regular basis until students *own* the words and use them effortlessly in their written and oral language.

Day 3: Stephanie knows (as discussed in chapter 1) that it takes between eight and fifteen repetitions before new information is mastered, so her routine involves additional review of the vocabulary words on the third day. This

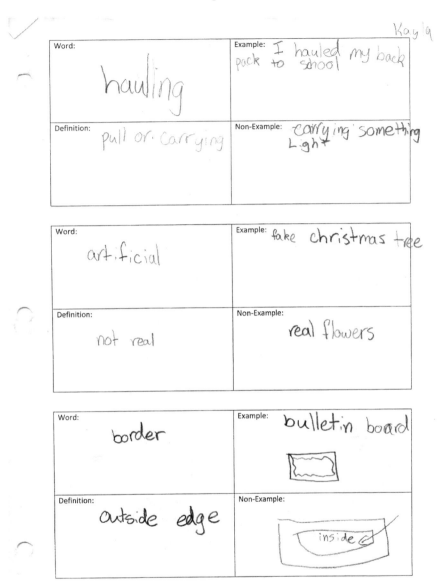

Kayla

| Word: | Example: I hauled my back pack to school |
|---|---|
| hauling | |
| Definition: pull or. carrying | Non-Example: carrying something Light |

| Word: | Example: fake christmas tree |
|---|---|
| artificial | |
| Definition: not real | Non-Example: real flowers |

| Word: | Example: bulletin board |
|---|---|
| border | |
| Definition: outside edge | Non-Example: inside |

**Figure 2.1.   Mental Organizer**

review varies, but one strategy the students especially enjoy is "I'm thinking of a word." Meeting with their partners, students give clues for which their partner must find a word. For example, one day Madison told her partner, "I'm thinking of a word that means you can hear loud music from the car next to you." Her partner Sam answered with the vocabulary word *blare*.

Sometimes "I'm thinking of a word" is acted out. One day Logan made a face. Jackson studied the vocabulary list and exclaimed, "Glowered!" Another time Eden said, "I thinking of a word that describes how I listen to my teacher." She then sat up straight and focused her attention to the front of the room. Her partner, Atira, located the word *attentively* on the list.

Day 4: By the fourth day the class has read and discussed the story, including the context of the new vocabulary words. On this day the class discusses any additional unknown words that came up in their reading. On day 4 the class also reviews the definition for each word in preparation for the weekly test that accompanies the basal program.

Day 5: By the time testing day rolls around, students have studied the words multiple times and in multiple ways. Students nearly always do well on the tests because of repeated exposure to the words in various contexts.

Apart from test scores, Stephanie knows the vocabulary routine is working because students regularly find words from their vocabulary lists while they are reading independently. Recently Grace approached Stephanie with book in hand. "Oh, look! Do you remember we talked about this word?" Grace exclaimed pointing to the word *immense*. Stephanie replied, "Yes. I do remember. Do you remember what it means?" Grace responded, "Really big!"

## STEPHANIE MURPHY'S FAVORITE: STORY IMPRESSIONS

One effective vocabulary strategy Stephanie uses in addition to the routines described above is "story impressions" (McGinley & Denner, 1987). Students are given a list of vocabulary words or short phrases taken directly from a text they will be reading. The words are listed down the left side of the page. On the right side of the page students write what they think the story will be about, using the words in the order they are listed. Students sometimes work independently and sometimes in pairs or teams to create their story impressions. Before actually reading the story, they share what they wrote. After reading the text, students revisit their story impression, compare and contrast it with the text, and write a summary of the actual story.

## CONCLUSION

In the following chapters you will read about vocabulary strategies that other teachers use routinely. You are probably already doing some of them; others may be new to you. Don't try to do them all. Follow Stephanie Murphy's lead and choose a few that you can do on a regular basis. You might want to establish a five-day plan that you follow all year as Stephanie does, or you might decide on a routine that changes from time to time. Having a routine doesn't mean you can't add other strategies. The important thing is to have a set of instructional strategies you use on a regular basis that are effective and that students know well so that teaching time and learning time are maximized.

## REFLECTION AND ACTION

The following questions are designed to help you think through your vocabulary instruction, either alone or with a group of colleagues. The reflection you do is an important part of reading the chapter. The action that results is what puts you among the ranks of great literacy teachers.

1. Tell about a time in your classroom when a disrupted routine resulted in learning being lost.
2. What routines do you have in place for vocabulary instruction?
3. Do you think students get bored with routines? What evidence can you cite to support your position?
4. Locate three graphic organizers that could be used for vocabulary instruction and share them with your discussion group. (A Google search will yield plenty of examples.)
5. What is one thing from this chapter that you would like to include in your own classroom?

*Chapter Three*

# You Don't Have to Be Greek to Teach Greek and Latin Roots!

If you knew that teaching a small list of words would have a significant impact on your students' reading, would you teach those words? Of course you would! Then consider this fact: well over half of English words are derived from Greek and Latin. By teaching a small list of Greek and Latin roots you will give students a powerful tool for analyzing the meanings of new words they encounter in conversation and in print.

A root is any word part that holds meaning. There are three kinds of roots: bases, prefixes, and suffixes. Three simple principles can help you plan instruction of roots:

1. A base is a root that provides the word's main meaning.
2. A prefix is a root placed at the beginning of a word.
3. A suffix is a root placed at the ending of a word.

Consider the words you can understand if you know just a few Greek and Latin roots.

Greek base: *scope*, meaning "to view," helps you analyze words such as *periscope*, *microscope*, and *telescope*.

Latin base: *dict*, meaning "to speak," helps you analyze words such as *dictation*, *dictate*, *dictator*, and *contradict*.

Greek prefix: *anti*, meaning "against" or "opposite," helps you analyze words such as *antivirus*, *antipodes*, and *antiwar*.

Latin prefix: *ab*, meaning "apart" or "away from," helps you analyze words such as *abnormal*, *abdicate*, and *abduct*.

Greek suffix: *ology*, meaning "study of," helps you analyze words such as *biology*, *psychology*, and *theology*.

Latin suffix: *able*, meaning "capable" or "worthy of," helps you analyze words such as *likable*, *manageable*, *fixable*.

As students learn more and more Greek and Latin bases and affixes, word analysis becomes a grand puzzle to be solved. Morphology, the study of the structure of language, provides instruction that is interesting, challenging, and effective.

## MORPHOLOGY INSTRUCTION
## IN FAIRFAX COUNTY, VIRGINIA

Joanna Newton is of Greek American heritage. She attended a Greek language and cultural school on Saturday mornings as a child, took Greek and Latin in high school, and took several languages in college. However, when she first began teaching third graders, she had no specific plan to use a Greek and Latin roots approach to vocabulary instruction. "I was looking for connections," she explained, "and that's what I know."

What Joanna knows about Greek and Latin roots has served her students well. Joanna also knows firsthand that teachers don't need a language background such as hers to help students use bases, prefixes, and suffixes as a springboard to vocabulary acquisition.

At the time this chapter was written Joanna had recently started her position as reading specialist at Mount Eagle Elementary School in Fairfax County, Virginia. She previously taught second and third graders at Fairfax's Groveton Elementary School. Joanna's story here is mostly about her position at Groveton. Her success with teaching reading there, particularly her vocabulary instruction, was instrumental in securing her the new position where 70 percent of her time is spent coaching/working with teachers and 30 percent working with students.

Groveton Elementary School is a Title I school (as is Mount Eagle Elementary where she now works). Groveton has a large population of English language learners (ELLs), mainly Hispanic, Pakistani, and West African. African Americans make up 38 percent of the student population, Hispanics 32 percent, and whites 15 percent, with the remainder from a variety of countries. "In our school vocabulary is a very big need," Joanna declared. "We need to give our students the background to get started."

## FINDING THE CONNECTION

Early in Joanna's first year of teaching, she was searching for a way to help students learn the vocabulary for a unit on the food chain. She described what happened.

> One day when I was teaching about omnivores, carnivores, and herbivores, I remembered that *vor* is a Latin root that means "to eat," so I told the students that. Then I said, "Oh! Those of you who know Spanish know that *carne* means 'meat.' So what would *carnivore* mean?" They made the connection right away. It was powerful. It was, "Ah!" for the kids *and* for me!
>
> I kept using this approach on an impromptu basis as needed; for example, I taught the Latin prefix *peri* (around) when we were studying perimeter in math. It was fun, made sense, and the students really seemed to get it, so soon it became my main approach to teaching vocabulary.

Joanna believes the most important criteria for vocabulary instruction is that it be meaning based. She commented that in the primary grades word work is often focused on word attack skills or spelling. "That's not *vocabulary*," she says. "That won't unlock the meaning. Students need that, but they need a lot more. If they don't know the meaning of the words they decode, then they're stuck—in comprehension and in writing."

Joanna now uses *Building Vocabulary from Word Roots* (Rasinski, Padak, Newton, & Newton, 2007). The program provides lesson plans and student activities, and Joanna finds it gives her vocabulary instruction "more structure." However, you don't have to purchase a program to have a word roots approach to vocabulary instruction. A search on the Internet will yield hundreds of common and not-so-common roots. (A recent Google search using the phrase "root words" resulted in 8,670,000 hits.) Most likely, you know more roots than you realize. Start with the ones you know, and incorporate some of Joanna's excellent ideas that follow. You'll find you don't have to be Greek to teach Greek and Latin roots!

## EXPANDING THE WORD ROOTS
## APPROACH INTO OTHER CLASSROOMS

The third-grade teachers at Groveton Elementary worked as a literacy team. They administered the vocabulary assessment from *Words Their Way* (Bear,

Invernizzi, Templeton, & Johnston, 2008). Students were grouped based on their needs into vocabulary study groups with each teacher taking a group for their targeted word study once a week. Joanna taught the highest group and began teaching them word roots immediately. The students still learned phonics and word patterns, but they were also building their vocabularies. Other staff members began to take note. Joanna talked about their interest.

> The reading teacher was very interested. She saw it in action with my students. Their writing samples were strong. The principal took an interest because he observed a roots-based approach being used at a nearby gifted and talented school. He saw the value of exposing our Title I students to high-level language. At that time there was no focused vocabulary program in the school.

Joanna, the reading teacher, and the principal encouraged other teachers to try it with their students, but there were obstacles of perception to overcome. Joanna explained,

> We had to spend some time getting over the notion that Greek and Latin roots are for older students or "smart kids." Strong readers and writers are going to get a meaning-based approach, but struggling readers rarely get there. They can do it. All students come with some understanding of base words.
>
> Some teachers felt this approach would be hard for ELLs. But we were missing a major point of entry, especially for Hispanic students because over 90 percent of English words with two or more syllables are Latin-based. Sometimes we feel our ELLs can only handle simple English, but this approach builds on their background knowledge. I tell teachers, "It's only difficult if you don't teach it to them."

In addition to counterproductive perceptions about which students could benefit from this approach, many teachers felt uneasy about teaching this way. Joanna declared,

> It was a different approach, especially with the younger kids. Teachers would tell me, "You know it. I don't. It's easy for you. It's not easy for me." I got that a lot from teachers. I encouraged them to do the roots they knew or to use our curriculum and teach the required prefixes and suffixes then move into roots that commonly occur in content areas, like *bio* (life) (*biology, biography*) or *-cracy* (government by) (*democracy, aristocracy*).

With Joanna's available expertise, the principal's leadership, and the reading teacher's support, some teachers gradually started incorporating word roots into their vocabulary instruction. Joanna said the most important thing for teachers to do is realize it's OK if they are not experts.

Sometimes a teacher would come to me and say, "I'm not sure if this is a root." I wouldn't always know. We all need to know what to do when we're put on the spot without knowing the answer. That means getting out of your comfort zone. I would help them just like I help students. The number one question is: Does it make sense? It's the same approach we take with comprehension. If the root you're looking at doesn't make sense, then it's probably a false etymology.

In Joanna's last year at Groveton, ten teachers used *Building Vocabulary from Word Roots* (Rasinski, Padak, Newton, & Newton, 2007). Pre- and posttests showed students jumping multiple levels. Several teachers noted that students were moving more on the *Words Their Way* continuum (Bear, Invernizzi, Templeton, & Johnston, 2008) than in past years. Joanna would like to gather more correlational data, and she hopes her new position will provide opportunities for her to do that.

## VOCABULARY ROUTINES

### Independent Reading

Like the other teachers in this book, Joanna strongly believes that independent reading builds vocabulary. Her students have a half hour of independent reading every day after recess. Often she provides highlighting tape, and students look for base words, prefixes, or suffixes as they are reading. When they gather for sharing, they discuss the words they found.

To ensure success during independent reading, Joanna administers an interest inventory at the beginning of the year and interviews each student about his/her reading interests, perceived strengths, and goals. Both the inventory and the interview questions are taken from *Practical Assessments for Literature-Based Reading Classrooms* (Fiderer, 1995). She uses this information to make suggestions for independent reading.

Joanna creates reading baskets to assure students' success. Each table group shares a basket of books that match the interests and reading levels of students who sit at that table. Students also get books during guided reading instruction that they can read during independent reading. Every quarter when Joanna changes her guided reading groups, she updates the baskets with books that match the students' reading levels. However, students are not limited to these books; they are free to choose any books they want from the classroom library.

### Classroom Talk

Joanna knows the research about involving children in conversations to build their vocabularies. "I try not to talk any differently to my students than I do to adults," she claimed. "I try to use big words with them. I use the term *false etymology* with them just like I do with the teachers." When she sets up independent reading, Joanna talks about *sustainability*—that good readers can *sustain* their reading for a long time. "I tell my students if they want to work on *sustaining* their reading, independent reading is a good time to practice." Subsequently, some students write *sustainability* as one of their reading goals.

Joanna also reads sophisticated poetry aloud. She explained,

> I try not to read just kids' poems. I read from poets like Langston Hughes and Adrienne Rich. At first the students are a little intimidated, but they love that they are doing something grown up. We go through the poem line by line and discuss the words they don't know. Then they write a response or sometimes they draw. They get excited about responding to the poem.

Sometimes parents verify that children are beginning to own their new words when they report how their child used a particular vocabulary word at home. Joanna laughs, "Parents get a kick out of it when their child tattles that his brother is being inhumane."

## WOW Words

Another vocabulary routine Joanna incorporates into her classroom is WOW words. Joanna tells her students to look for words in their reading or listen for words they hear during read aloud that make them say, "WOW!" After reading, the class discusses the words and puts them on the WOW bulletin board. Of course, Joanna then encourages them to use the WOW words in their conversations or writing.

## JOANNA NEWTON'S FAVORITE: ROOT OF THE WEEK

Each week Joanna's students study a specific word root, and that helps them learn how to break words down to find their meanings. The heart of the lesson is "meet the root" where students "divide and conquer" a list of ten words as they identify base words, prefixes, and suffixes (Rasinski, Padak, Newton, & Newton, 2007). For example, students might study the root *trac*, learning that it means "to pull, draw, or drag." Then they examine words like *tractor*, *track*, and *retractable* (see figure 3.1).

It's essential that students use the words in meaningful contexts, so Joanna plans a variety of activities to assure they do. Each day Joanna leads the students in fifteen minutes of wordplay using their newly acquired vocabulary. The students especially enjoy riddles. To go along with the *trac* example,

**Part A:**
Meet the Root    *Elijah*

# Divide and Conquer

**Directions:** "Divide" words and then "conquer" them by writing the meaning of the words. Remember that *trac* and *tract* mean "pull, draw, drag." An X means the word does not have a prefix.

| | prefix means | base means | word means |
|---|---|---|---|
| 1. tractor | X | Pull | a machine that pulls dirt |
| 2. contract | with, together | Pull | to pull something together |
| 3. retract | back | Pull or draw | Pull back, withdraw |
| 4. attract | to, toward | Pull, draw | to pull something |
| 5. subtract | under | Pull | to pull under |
| 6. extract | out | Pull, draw | to pull or draw out |
| 7. detract | down | Pull, draw | to pull down |
| 8. distraction | in different directions | Pull, draw | to pull attention away from something |
| 9. attractive | to, forward | draw | to be drawn toward something |
| 10. retrace | back again | draw | to draw again |

**Figure 3.1.   Meet the Root: Divide and Conquer. Reprinted with permission from Teacher Created Materials.**

Joanna gave the following riddle: I am a pen that pulls back into itself. Previously her students had learned the prefix *re* and the suffix *able*, so they were able to come up with the word *retractable*. "I don't worry too much about whether they remember the complete word. What's important is that they learn the root so that they can apply it later. I want them to learn how to look at words differently."

At times students make up their own riddles. Sometimes they use base words, prefixes, and suffixes correctly, but the word they come up with is not correct. For example, Mario made the following riddle: I am a teacher who teaches you how to forget what you learned. Who am I? *An unteacher.* Ashly wrote: I am what babies do before they walk. What am I? *Prewalk.*

Joanna advises that teachers honor the attempts students make when learning with this approach to vocabulary. Anthony made up the word *tricentipede* in his writing. Joanna said, "When I asked him about it he said it is a bug with 300 legs. I responded, 'That bug doesn't exist but that could be what we called it if there were bugs like that.'"

Joanna also creates a weekly "graffiti board" to encourage students to find the root of the week in their reading. She places a large sheet of butcher paper on the wall. During the week when students find words with the root of the week, they jot them on the paper along with their initials. On Friday the class discusses all the words they found. Figure 3.2 shows the graffiti board for the roots *peri* and *graph*.

Joanna also looks for poetry that contains a word root. She copies the poem on chart paper, and the class reads it together several times. The poem then goes to the fluency center where students engage in repeated reading all week. Sometimes Joanna and the students use prefixes and suffixes to write a *copy change* of the poem. For example, they rewrote the poem "The Friendly Monster" (Hajdusiewicz, 1999) into "The Unfriendly Monster."

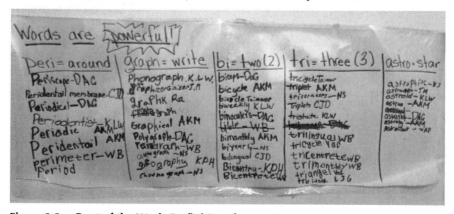

**Figure 3.2.   Root of the Week Grafitti Board.**

The class also has a song of the week, often related to a content area that contains the word root. Joanna finds some songs on the Internet and makes some up. Sometimes she takes an old favorite and tweaks it to include the word root.

## CONCLUSION

Joanna feels strongly that explicit vocabulary instruction is as integral to language arts instruction as reading and writing. However, she faces the same concern that all teachers face in an age of high-stakes accountability. She lamented,

> Sometimes it's hard because of the tests. We're under so much pressure to get through the curriculum and have time left over for test prep. It can be hard to find time for vocabulary instruction. It can also be challenging because unlike reading and writing, there's no systematic way to measure vocabulary. It's just the nature of words; they have multiple meanings and are used in multiple contexts. As teachers we're held accountable for demonstrating student progress. We have to show that our students have improved $x$ many levels in reading and that they have mastered specific skills in their writing assessments.
>
> We don't have a systematic way to measure or demonstrate students' vocabulary growth. So when your time is limited and the pressure is on, sometimes you have to focus on the areas that you have to turn in data for, which means spending less time on vocabulary. It can really be counterproductive though, because the more vocabulary students know the better they will do on standardized tests, writing assessments, and reading.

Joanna has this advice for teachers who want to try the Greek and Latin roots approach to vocabulary:

> Don't be afraid. Let yourself learn along with the kids. I think we have to give ourselves permission to be learners as well as teachers. We don't have to be experts at everything. I think we can show our students that we are learning too, that learning doesn't stop when you are a grown up. In fact I think it's a good way to model curiosity and problem solving. Be honest. Say, "I don't know," if you don't know—and then figure it out!

## REFLECTION AND ACTION

The following questions are designed to help you think through your vocabulary instruction, either alone or with a group of colleagues. The reflection you do is an important part of reading the chapter. The action that results is what puts you among the ranks of great literacy teachers.

1. To what extent do you teach base words, prefixes, and suffixes in your classroom?
2. What is your biggest concern regarding this approach to vocabulary instruction?
3. How did you learn word meanings when you were in school? What grade were you in when teachers introduced prefixes, suffixes, and base words?
4. Make a list of all the prefixes and suffixes you can think of. Look in a resource book or on the Internet for some others you know but perhaps forgot about.
5. Have you encountered "obstacles of perception" in your school (whether related or unrelated to word roots)? What were those perceptions? Use the following "focused free write" meeting procedure to explore this question.
6. What is one thing from this chapter that you would like to include in your own classroom?

## MEETING PROCEDURE: FOCUSED FREE WRITE

Purpose:            Provides the opportunity to synthesize ideas or reactions
Advantage:          Everyone participates
                    Generates reflective conversation
Disadvantage:       Some participants can be uncomfortable putting their comments in writing
Steps:

1. Participants respond to a topic, question, or statement. For this free write use question 5 in "Reflection and Action."
2. Participants write for a specified length of time without stopping, usually four or five minutes.
3. Participants may not stop writing. If they get to a point where they can't think of anything else to say, they repeat the last phrase or sentence until another thought comes.
4. When time is up, ask for volunteers to read what they have written or collect the free writes and read several anonymously.

Meeting procedure adapted from:
   M. A. Forget (2004), *MAX Teaching with Reading and Writing: Classroom Activities for Helping Students Learn New Subject Matter While Acquiring Literacy Skills.*

## Chapter Four

# Creating a Classroom Context That Supports Vocabulary Instruction

Student success requires a classroom that is brimming with enthusiasm, curiosity, and risk-taking. Great teachers make that happen. Decades of research have documented the importance of parent involvement, but research has also shown that when parent involvement is lacking, great teachers can still make a difference. Studies have repeatedly indicated a correlation between financial means and student achievement, but studies have also found that great teachers can make a difference, even in the face of poverty. In recent decades the achievement gap seems to be dominated by minority students, but data show the achievement gap narrows when a great teacher is present.

Indeed, William Sanders, who has spent several decades studying factors that impact student achievement, concluded:

- Teacher effectiveness is the single biggest factor influencing gains in achievement, an influence many times greater than poverty or per-pupil expenditure.
- A teacher's impact on student learning lingers up to four years.
- Having a high-quality teacher throughout elementary school can substantially offset or even eliminate the disadvantage of low-socioeconomic background (Sanders & Rivers, 1996).

When it comes to vocabulary instruction, great teachers make a difference.

## ESTABLISHING A CULTURE THAT ALL STUDENTS DESERVE IN SHAWNEE, KANSAS

In 2008 Jeri Powers was teacher of the year for the state of Kansas. It's easy to see why. Ask Jeri about teaching and her voice crackles with passion, like a live wire. There will be no conversations about vocabulary routines, instructional strategies, or "what works" until she's had her say about what comes first: creating the classroom culture that *all* students deserve. Then, and only then, will Jeri tell you about her vocabulary instruction.

Jeri is a grades K–5 reading specialist at Riverview Elementary School in Shawnee, Kansas. Shawnee's student population is diverse, and Jeri's school is on the affluent side of town. Many of the district's elementary-aged English language learners (ELLs) are bused to Riverview. Although their numbers are small, they represent twelve countries. "That's a lot of different languages," Jeri observed. "Some are adopted from other countries and come from homes where education is valued."

In describing Riverview's students Jeri acknowledged, "Our students come to school with strong background knowledge." Even so, Riverview Elementary has its share of students who struggle with reading. And how does Jeri, as a reading specialist, teach them? By first establishing the classroom culture that *all* students need and deserve, whether they are struggling or proficient readers; children of affluence or poverty; ELLs or native English speakers; elementary students or high school students—in effect *all* students.

## Teacher Attitude and Enthusiasm

In Jeri's estimation there is one element that trumps all others in establishing a classroom where students are excited about reading and writing—the teacher's attitude and enthusiasm. She declared emphatically,

> The teacher must be curious, want to learn, love words. If they see you loving language they will love it, too. When it comes to vocabulary, you have to love words. Although the strategies are important, if you aren't creating the culture that says words are important, and if you're not excited about it, it's just paper.

But being excited isn't enough. She explained,

> I'm sometimes surprised to learn some teachers don't read much professionally. We have to keep learning, and we have to be sure the students know we are learners and we are excited about it. Teachers need to take classes, share ideas, talk with colleagues. (See chapter 10 for more on professional development and vocabulary instruction.)

Jeri believes the extent to which students feel safe is an important component of a strong classroom culture. It is imperative that the teacher model that safety by saying, "I don't know" when it needs to be said. In terms of vocabulary Jeri says, "Students have to feel it's OK to say, 'I don't know that word.'"

Such an acknowledgment can be modeled by the teacher during the sharing that follows independent reading. (As pointed out in chapter 1, teachers also need to read when students read independently and share what they have been reading.) Independent reading is a good time for the teacher to consciously look for words that are new to her. It might even be necessary to seek out a book for the next independent reading time that contains a new word or two so that such modeling is not left to chance.

Jeri also believes the classroom culture should allow students to be risk-takers. Students need to be willing to read texts with more difficult words and to approach new words with a sense of "fun and wonder." As you might guess by now, Jeri feels strongly that risk-taking begins with the teacher. She stated,

> The teacher has to be a risk-taker. On a professional level, she needs to be willing to go beyond the teacher's manual. Our core program has many vocabulary activities, but it can't always be what the guide says to do. It isn't always in your lesson plans. It just happens as you're watching kids. For example, one day we were watching a National Geographic film about water-holding frogs and I heard the word *burrow*. That's the time for a vocabulary lesson even if *burrow* isn't on their list of words for the thematic unit we are doing.

In chapter 1 we looked at Mary Budd Rowe's seminal research on classroom discussions (Rowe, 1972). As you will recall, Rowe concluded that students need more wait time than they are often given in classrooms. Jeri echoed this conclusion.

> In establishing a supportive culture, we need to give them time to think. Some kids need time for processing. They need for us to just shut up. I often say to students, "Do you need my coaching or time?" It's surprising how many say, "Time." We just assume they don't know and can't figure it out, and so we tell them. Or we tend to pay attention to the students who are blurting out, and then others don't get a chance to talk—to develop vocabulary.

Jeri shared that during her year as Kansas teacher of the year she was distressed by how often people suggested that struggling learners need the best teachers. She stated her philosophy:

> *All* kids deserve great teachers. Money doesn't buy your problems away. Great teachers are excited about learning. They want so much for the kids to be excited, too. Establishing the culture—that's the fun part—the way that culture is cultivated is through you. When you're having fun teaching, that's when they want to come to school.

## JERI POWERS'S STUDENTS

Riverview Elementary School uses the response to intervention (RTI) model to determine the needs of students. The RTI model places students into one of three levels for instruction, assessment, and interventions. The first level, or tier I, is for the majority of students (about 75–80 percent) who will benefit from a high-quality, general education. The second level, or tier II, is for a smaller percentage of students (10–15 percent) who are considered at risk and will require support beyond tier I in order to be successful. Tier III includes the smallest percentage of students (5–10 percent), those who are not responding sufficiently to interventions in tier II.

Every student in Riverview Elementary School is assessed in the fall with several measures including Dynamic Indicators of Basic Early Literacy Skills (DIBELS) (Good & Kaminski, 2001) and MAP (Measures of Academic Performance). Students with low scores are administered the Diagnostic Assessment of Reading (DAR) (Chall, Curtis, Curtis, & Kearns, 2005) as one component of determining which tier of support they need. Results are used to guide intervention plans.

Jeri mostly works with tier III students. She teaches in a variety of contexts. Some of her students receive one-on-one instruction while others work with Jeri in small groups. She also provides large group instruction as she co-

**Figure 4.1. Jeri Power's Students**

teaches in some classrooms. She explained that she is doing more and more coteaching lately.

> We do whatever is necessary, but we're coming to believe more and more that if I only do intervention, we'll never address the core reading instruction, which must be strong for *all* students. If I don't spend at least some of my day collaborating with teachers to strengthen our core instruction, my tier (III) caseload will be overflowing.

Jeri made the following connection between tier III students and vocabulary acquisition:

> We've talked a lot about this in our building. When we have students who are weak in vocabulary, they stand out. Do they stand out because others are so high or because there is a problem? But we find these are the kids who struggle, and their struggles show up in reading comprehension. That's not surprising since we know how comprehension and vocabulary are connected. They just don't have the words so they say generic words—*stuff, things*. So we have to decide how to help them build their vocabulary.

## VOCABULARY ROUTINES

### Independent Reading

Jeri has established a set of regular routines to help her struggling readers. She knows that elementary students encounter unknown words nearly every time they pick up a new book. Having established a culture that encourages students to say, "I don't know that word," provides the context for them to learn the meanings of those new words.

Every day all students in the school have twenty to thirty minutes of independent reading. During this time Jeri's students may choose to read alone or with a buddy. If they choose to buddy read there is an established procedure for implementing that choice:

1. Put your name on the board.
2. Return to your reading spot and read quietly.
3. If you want to buddy read with someone, go to the board and cross off the name at the top of the list. That is your reading buddy for the day.
4. Go to a place where you won't disturb others.
5. Take turns reading, either the same book or your own books.
6. Help each other when needed.
7. Talk about what you read.

As with all classroom routines, this procedure requires much teacher-directed modeling. Jeri told of one teacher who was preparing to implement regular independent reading time in her classroom. She asked another teacher who had an established independent reading time if she and her students could walk through to see what a class looks like when it is engaged in reading.

Later in the day, the teacher of the model classroom complimented her class on how well they demonstrated independent reading time for the other class. The students looked a bit confused, until finally one student asked, "Someone walked in?" The students had been so engaged in reading that they didn't even notice visitors walking through their class. Jeri pointed out, "This didn't happen without a *ton* of modeling, clear teacher expectations, and practice, practice, practice of what independent reading should look, sound, and feel like."

Jeri knows that quality conversations lead to vocabulary development, so sharing is not an add-on to independent reading but an essential component. Students are encouraged to talk about their books as they read with a buddy. "I have observed them talk about the meanings of words so many times. One student will say, 'Do you know what that means?' and the other will explain the word." In addition, at the conclusion of independent reading time, students "turn and talk" to someone near them about what they read and any new words they encountered. "Conversations lead your instruction," Jeri declared.

## Writing

Jeri believes students learn new vocabulary through writing, so her students write every day. However, unlike gaining some understanding of words from context, building vocabulary through writing requires direct teacher instruction. Jeri conducts writing conferences with students in small groups or one-on-one. Marilee, known for overusing the word *thing*, was writing a piece about water-holding frogs. Jeri noticed she was struggling to find words so Jeri began "implanting new words."

> I asked her if she knew what an amphibian was. We went to the computer and did a search. The Internet is so helpful! Then I asked her to describe how she thinks an amphibian feels. She said, "It's slimy." So she had two good words to replace the word *thing*—slimy amphibian. When I do this kind of scaffolding I have to ask myself, "Is this really a word they're going to need?" One day we were reading a book about mummification. I decided not to spend much time on *sarcophagus* because it is such a rarely used word.
>
> They lead the way. I plan ahead and select vocabulary words that I think will need to be learned in order to comprehend the text; however, many times the words I select are not the ones students need and I must switch my instructional plan to meet their real needs. I have to have a plan, yet be flexible.

Jeri also helps her students incorporate words they've newly acquired in other contexts into their daily writing. After watching the National Geographic video on water-holding frogs, the students wrote about what they had learned. Cahill wrote, "It can dig its own hole in the dirt." Jeri pointed out that the hole was called a *burrow* in the video. Then she asked, "If you stepped in the dirt how do you think it would feel?" Cahill replied, "Wet and squishy." With a bit more scaffolding, Cahill's sentence read, "It can dig its own three-foot deep wet squishy hole called a burrow." Jeri pointed out, "When we get these kinds of sentences I project them on the SmartBoard as examples for other students. They have to dig deep to use their new vocabulary this way."

## Read Alouds

Jeri knows a carefully selected read aloud is bursting with opportunities to build vocabulary. She was reading *Because of Winn-Dixie* (DiCamillo, 2009) to her fourth-grade students. *Winn-Dixie* is packed with rich words that encourage visualization in the reader's mind. Sometimes, however, words and phrases that can so easily create mental images in some readers are a stumbling block for students who are unfamiliar with nonliteral phrases. Jeri used the conversations surrounding this read aloud to help her students whose vocabularies are very literal to build new connections.

For example, they discussed the following passage: "Winn-Dixie looked like a furry bullet, shooting across the building, chasing that mouse" (p. 36). They talked about what a bullet is, how it moves, and what message the author was trying to convey. Drawing pictures of the scene and how they individually imagined it helped each student to cement the scene in his or her mind.

## JERI POWERS'S FAVORITE: EXHAUSTED WORDS MAP

Jeri often uses a strategy called "exhausted words map" to help students build vocabulary. (Notice even the word *exhausted* is an attempt at extending vocabulary.) When Jeri read *Matilda* (Dahl, 1988) with a small group of students, she pointed out the word *chirruped* in following sentence: "'Yes, Miss Honey,' chirruped eighteen eager little voices" (p. 69). Jeri shared,

> That small sentence is full of language that so richly expresses the mood and atmosphere of this classroom scene. You can't read past it without seeing and feeling what it was like to be sitting in one of those eighteen chairs. How can a teacher read right past phrases such as this one without stopping to elicit some excitement and enjoyment?

Jeri modeled her enjoyment of words by the way she said *chirruped* . . . and said it . . . and said it. Madeline commented, "You really like that word, don't you?" Jeri explained that *chirruped* is such an interesting word compared to the word *said*, an exhausted word. She then led the group in creating a word map with words that could be used in place of *said* (see figure 4.3).

First they discussed how a character might be feeling when he or she said something. They came up with the words *happy, nervous, scared, angry,* and *cranky*. Then they looked for words to replace the word *said* with those feelings in mind. Of course, *chirruped* was the first word on the map, but the students also suggested words like *shrieked, yelled, scolded, told,* and *sang*. The next step was for the students to use the words from the word map in their own writing. "I tell them we have to use the words as an author would. We have to make the words we use pull the reader in."

Sometimes the "exhausted words map" activity is completed as a whole group activity, and sometimes students create their own exhausted words map. Jeri is ready to jump in with this strategy on an as-needed basis. Nate was writing about his brother and wrote, "When he hit me, it made me sad." Jeri asked, "Were you really sad? Or were you feeling something else? Let's make a map of all the words you could use instead of *sad*." Nate's exhausted words map included *angry, frustrated,* and *upset*.

**Figure 4.2.  Student Locating Words for Exhausted Words Map**

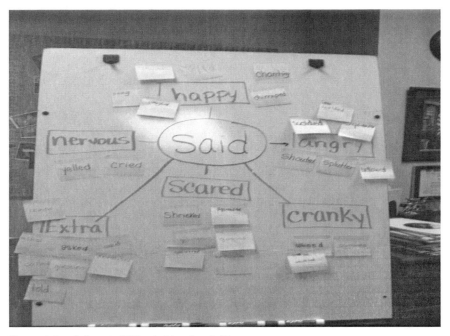

**Figure 4.3.   Exhausted Words Map for *Said***

## CONCLUSION

Jeri sometimes worries about how much vocabulary knowledge her struggling readers are acquiring. She pondered,

> Vocabulary is such a tricky thing. Monitoring vocabulary progress is difficult. What assessment is out there to show small increments of growth in overall vocabulary development? Students might perform well on a vocabulary test aligned with a unit of study; however, evidence to show if they transfer that knowledge beyond the test to their own writing and speaking is a much more complex process to assess and monitor.
>
> Is it transferring? How many times do I have to see the new word or hear it to know? I look for evidence. I take notes of things they've said, words they've used. I might write, "I didn't know he knew it, and he used it appropriately." I take these observation notes to the Tier II and Tier III Improvement Team.

Despite the ambiguity of assessing whether a student knows a word, Jeri feels confident that her students are making progress in their vocabulary acquisition because of the quality instruction she and her colleagues provide. In the end, though, Jeri returns to where she started: "If they are just putting words in their notebooks and you aren't creating an exciting vocabulary culture, it's not going anywhere."

## REFLECTION AND ACTION

The following questions are designed to help you think through your vocabulary instruction, either alone or with a group of colleagues. The reflection you do is an important part of reading the chapter. The action that results is what puts you among the ranks of great literacy teachers.

1. What do you do on a regular basis to establish a classroom culture that *all* students deserve?
2. What are the biggest obstacles to establishing a culture such as Jeri describes? What can teachers do to overcome those obstacles? With your discussion group, respond to this question using the meeting procedure, "consultation line," below.
3. Do you agree or disagree with the people who told Jeri that children in the lowest performing schools should have the best teachers? Why or why not?
4. What is one thing from this chapter that you do well?
5. What additional "words of wisdom" could you give for establishing a classroom culture that all students deserve?
6. Jeri said, "I'm sometimes surprised to learn some teachers don't read much professionally." Do you think that is true? If so, why do you think that is? If you don't think it is true, what is your evidence?
7. What is the last article or book you read that included ideas for vocabulary instruction? Share one idea from that reading with your colleagues.
8. What is one thing from this chapter that you would like to include in your own classroom?

## MEETING PROCEDURE: CONSULTATION LINE

| | |
|---|---|
| Purpose: | To receive advice from peers on a problem, question, or idea |
| Advantage: | Everyone in the group gets feedback from multiple perspectives |
| Disadvantage: | Some people may be asked to give advice on an issue for which they are not qualified |

Steps:

1. Each person in the group comes with an issue for which they would like input. (For purposes of this discussion, use question 2 in "Reflection and Action": What are the biggest obstacles in establishing classroom culture?)
2. Divide the participants into two equal groups Participants sit in two rows of chairs facing one another, knee to knee.
3. People in one row of chairs are designated as speakers; people in the other row are consultants.
4. The speaker tells the person directly across from him or her about the situation for which he or she would like advice. (In this instance, what the speaker thinks are the biggest obstacles in establishing classroom culture.)
5. The "consultant" makes suggestions, asks questions to help the speaker think it through, shares stories of his/her experiences with a similar issue, and so on.
6. After three minutes the consultation line moves down one chair. The person from the end of the line will fill in the empty chair that is created at the other end when everyone moves down one. Speakers stay in the same seat.
7. Repeat steps 4, 5, and 6.
8. The speaker will get advice from three different people.
9. Switch sides and repeat the process with the consultants now becoming the speakers.
10. Repeat steps 4, 5, and 6 three times.

## Chapter Five

# Vocabulary Strategies:
# Where to Look First

An old Egyptian proverb tells us, "When spiderwebs unite, they can tie up a lion." Imagine the "lions" that can be tied up when great teachers unite! When teachers who are committed, imaginative, and creative share instructional ideas and solve problems together, students become "ours" rather than "mine."

It's not unusual to hear teachers ask if they can "steal that idea." Most teachers don't worry about their ideas being "stolen." Teachers like to share what works for students. If you doubt that, do a Google search using the phrase *teacher-created lesson plans.* A recent search with that phrase yielded 107 million hits, and certainly that descriptor did not cover all the possibilities. In addition, some successful publishing companies have found their product line of "teacher-created materials" to be wildly popular.

Teachers love to peek into other classrooms, talk to colleagues, and go to workshops where they can learn what has worked for their peers. Then they take those teacher-tested ideas and adapt them to meet the needs of their own students. As you look to improve your vocabulary instruction, look to your colleagues first. That's what Jackie Zaucha does.

## EFFECTIVE VOCABULARY STRATEGIES
## LEARNED FROM COLLEAGUES IN STOW, OHIO

Jackie Zaucha considers collaboration with peers to be a critical aspect of teaching. "I have a close network of teachers and family members that I learn from," she explained.

Networking is my strength. I get ideas from the teachers in my school, my mother-in-law who is a teacher, and even from my husband who is a library media specialist at a local middle school. I always want to know what good teaching looks like in someone's classroom. I know there's no one right way. I want to get all the ideas I can so that I can see what works best for my students.

Through years of networking with colleagues, Jackie has developed a comprehensive literacy program for her struggling readers, which includes specific strategies for vocabulary acquisition. She involves families in vocabulary-building activities as often as possible.

Jackie teaches K–3 Title I students at Highland Elementary School in Stow, Ohio, primarily a white, middle-class "bedroom community." Although there is good parent involvement at Highland, Jackie finds many of her students have a vocabulary deficit. She revealed,

It seems like these days children spend their free time playing video games and watching TV. This does not allow for good conversations to take place at home. As soon as they walk into the room, I get them involved in everyday conversations—just talking about their day. Some children need to be reminded to talk in complete sentences. I often model this for them.

Jackie's students come to her with a strong phonics background. They usually know some comprehension strategies, but they frequently have to be reminded to use them. Vocabulary and fluency are areas where her students need a great deal of instruction. Of course their word recognition greatly impacts fluency as well as comprehension.

## VOCABULARY ROUTINES

### Awesome Words

Jackie and her students are constantly on the lookout for "awesome words." She instructs them to listen to conversations and pay attention to all kinds of print as they go about their daily activities. The students (and Jackie!) jot down "awesome words" they find and bring them to class to discuss. Students bring words they hear on the radio, on TV, within their video games, and in conversations with family and friends. Their print-based words come from sources such as cereal boxes, books, newspapers, road signs, Internet, and candy wrappers. There is never a lack of new words when students pay attention to print and conversations around them.

Students enjoy when Jackie gives them a stack of magazines and asks them to find some "awesome words." They cut words from the magazines and glue them in their journals. Beside each word they write a definition in their own words or draw a picture to illustrate the word. This involves a great deal of conversation as students scramble to find the meanings of their "awesome words." Students then gather in small groups, trade journals, and use one another's "awesome words" in sentences. Jackie described what sometimes happens. "I think the interesting part is when the word has multiple meanings and several students use the word in different ways." (See figures 5.1 and 5.2.)

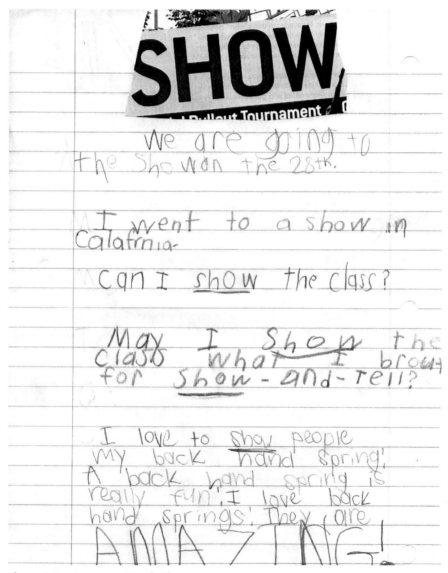

**Figure 5.1. Awesome Words-Show**

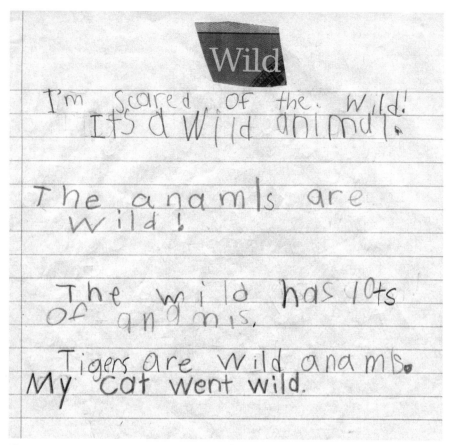

**Figure 5.2. Awesome Words—Wild**

Jackie encourages students to use their "awesome words" in their conversations and writing over time, and she praises them when they do.

### Family Involvement

Jackie uses the *Fast Start* family involvement program (Padak & Rasinski, 2005). The program is structured so that children take home one or two poems a week, including classic nursery rhymes, simple engaging poems, and poems that can be sung to familiar tunes. Families spend ten minutes per night with the *Fast Start* routine: (1) Read to your child; (2) r0ead with your child; and (3) listen to your child read. Family pages direct families to play with words from the poems (e.g., clap syllables as a stanza is read; locate rhyming words; play word concentration, go fish, or word bingo; find compound words; find suffixes; find word families; and so on).

*Fast Start* is a commercial program, but you can create a similar program of your own. You will need poems or songs and some strategies for working with words. Question 3 in the "Reflection and Action" section at the end of this chapter will get you started.

## Note Card Summaries

Jackie doesn't always preteach vocabulary. "Sometimes we spend a lot of time preteaching vocabulary when they could get most of the words from context clues," she explained. (See chapter 6 for more on context clues.) When she thinks the text provides enough context for figuring out new words, Jackie asks the students to locate words that are interesting or new to them. Everyone then writes his or her words on note cards and places them in the middle of the table. Students help one another with any word someone couldn't figure out from context clues.

One day, for example, a group of students was reading a passage about emperor penguins. Several students wrote the word *krill* on their note cards and indicated that they still didn't know what the word meant. Brandon offered, "It must be some kind of fish because penguins like to eat fish." Jackie then helped the students look up the word on the Internet so that they could see what *krill* look like.

After students discuss the pile of note cards, they each pick three to five of the words to use in writing a summary of what they read. They keep their own note cards and refer to them later for reading or writing.

## JACKIE ZAUCHA'S FAVORITE: WORD LADDERS

Jackie loves to use word ladders to build vocabulary, and her students and their parents love them, too. Word ladders allow students to build and examine words. To begin a word ladder, students draw a ladder with as many rungs as the teacher indicates. Rungs are numbered from bottom to top, with number 1 being at the bottom. Then the teacher guides students in "climbing the ladder" by giving them clues for making a new word for each rung of the ladder. Ideally, the first and last words are related in some way. Figure 5.3 shows a word ladder for a unit on marine life.

Jackie uses premade word ladders (Rasinski, 2008), but it's also fun to create your own. When students have had ample time to use word ladders, they often become good at creating their own. At the end of this chapter you will find a template you or your students can use for creating your own word ladders.

Jackie's students take a word ladder home once a week for parent involvement. It's a popular homework assignment. Isabelle reported, "My mom

| Clues | Letter Changes Required | Target Word |
|---|---|---|
| A word to describe animals that live in the sea | Put an r in the middle of the word you just made and you will have the secret word | 9. Marine |
| The name of a state | Add a vowel | 8. Maine |
| The most important idea | Change a letter | 7. Main |
| Something that falls from the sky | Add a vowel | 6. Rain |
| You went very fast with your legs | Change a letter | 5. Ran |
| Only one man | Change the vowel | 4. Man |
| More than one man | Add a letter | 3. Men |
| A word I use when talking about myself. | Change the first letter and take off the final vowel | 2. Me |
| A synonym for the ocean | Use three letters | 1. Sea |

**Figure 5.3. Word Ladder: From *Sea* to *Marine***

can't wait for those word ladders to come home." When students bring their completed word ladders back to school, Jackie uses the words from the ladders in other vocabulary-building activities. Sometimes they do word sorts, with Jackie giving clues such as the following: Which words on the ladder express what a person can do or feel? Which words on the ladder are nouns? Which words on the ladder have short vowels? Which words on the ladder were new to you?

## CONCLUSION

Of course Jackie also uses time-tested routines such as read alouds, word walls, and independent reading to build students' vocabularies. Because

Jackie works in a district where parent involvement is the norm, she often gets notes from parents about how pleased they are with their child's reading progress. "The notes aren't specifically about vocabulary," Jackie states, "but we know without developing vocabulary they aren't going to become good readers."

"I am interested in trying new ideas," Jackie claims. "I believe when a teacher is enthusiastic about a lesson the children will learn more." Jackie's strength in networking with colleagues has paid off with many new ideas and successes for her students.

Note: At the time of Jackie Zaucha's interview, she had accepted a new position on the previous day. She now teaches second grade at St. Joseph's School in Cuyahoga Falls, Ohio. This chapter is based on her experience as a Title I teacher in Stow, Ohio.

## REFLECTION AND ACTION

The following questions are designed to help you think through your vocabulary instruction, either alone or with a group of colleagues. The reflection you do is an important part of reading the chapter. The action that results is what puts you among the ranks of great literacy teachers.

1. Find five "awesome words" this week. Be creative when looking for words. Share the words with your discussion group. (1) Where did you find the word (e.g., novel, picture book, magazine article, brochure, menu, advertisement, website, letter, billboard, food package, directions, catalog, cartoon, conversation, etc.)? (2) Give a definition for the word. (3) Why is it an awesome word?
2. Make a word ladder for a social studies or science concept your students study.
3. Jackie Zaucha said, "I always want to know what good teaching looks like in someone's classroom." Do you know what good teaching looks like in classrooms in your school? Schedule some time to visit another classroom. Take notes on great literacy instruction and share what you learned with your discussion group.
4. Choose a familiar children's poem or song for your discussion group to work with. Develop family involvement activities related to vocabulary to go with the poem or song. Think about how you could expand this idea for family involvement in vocabulary development.
5. What is one thing from this chapter that you would like to include in your own classroom?

# TEMPLATE FOR PLANNING A WORD LADDER

From _____ to _____

| Clues | Letter Changes Required | Target Word |
|---|---|---|
|  |  | 8. |
|  |  | 7. |
|  |  | 6. |
|  |  | 5. |
|  |  | 4. |
|  |  | 3. |
|  |  | 2. |
|  |  | 1. |

Use the template to write clues for a "*read* to *learn*" word ladder.
Note: This idea was provided by Dr. Timothy Rasinski (personal communication, August 23, 2010).

read
real
zeal
heal
head
lead
lean
learn

Read to Learn!

## Chapter Six

# Be an Active Decision Maker When Planning Vocabulary Instruction

*Standards*, *testing*, and *accountability* are arguably three words that best describe the current state of American education. When you sign a contract to teach in a district, you are agreeing to teach the district-adopted curriculum. You cannot teach a topic just because you're interested in it or you think the students would enjoy it. You may know that your students love dinosaurs, but unless it is in your grade-level curriculum, you cannot teach a unit on dinosaurs. You may think your students should know about the Holocaust, but unless it is in your grade-level curriculum, you may not teach the Holocaust.

Although standards and testing are often blamed for taking away teacher creativity, such requirements are not all bad. In years past, when teachers were not so limited in what they could teach, there was often duplication of topics from year to year. For example, all kids love dinosaurs so it was not unusual for dinosaurs to be taught in kindergarten, then in first grade, and maybe again in third grade or fourth grade. Such duplication does not make the best use of students' learning time. Or a teacher might decide to teach slavery at the second- or third-grade level, a topic that is not developmentally appropriate for young students.

To compound the problem, students often ended up with gaps in their education because there may have been topics students needed to learn, but no teacher chose to teach. Conceivably, students could leave elementary school never having been taught, for example, the solar system or geography of the United States. Another problem was that students who transferred from one district to another often had very different school experiences and could be either far advanced above, or far behind, their new classmates.

The most recent standards initiative is the national common core standards. To date, common core standards have been developed for mathematics and English language arts. At the time this chapter was written, forty-five states

51

had officially adopted the common core standards. Assessments, which will eventually replace state tests, are currently being developed to go along with the common core standards.

Standards and accountability are important; *however*, so is the teacher as a decision maker! Honor the requirements, but remember you are the teacher who is with the students day in and day out, and you, more than anyone else, know what they need instructionally. Be an active decision maker when it comes to planning vocabulary instruction.

## VOCABULARY INSTRUCTION WITHIN THE CONTEXT OF STANDARDS, TESTS, AND ACCOUNTABILITY IN BALTIMORE, MARYLAND

Jill Johnson-McMullen is a creative reading teacher who faces the same requirements you probably face: state standards, a structured local curriculum, and high-stakes tests. She honors those commitments. "Everything I teach will be based on state standards," she promises. Then she adds with a smile, "But I'll do it my way" . . . and that works well for her students!

Jill teaches sixth grade reading at Murray Hill Middle School in the Howard County Public School System. The school is in Laurel, Maryland, an area Jill describes as "suburban with an urban feel." Being just thirty miles north of Washington, DC, those in the area cannot escape the big city context. Forty-five percent of Murray Hill's student population is African American, and 18 percent is Hispanic. There is a free and reduced lunch rate of 28 percent.

Although Jill's school physically sits in the midst of a wealthy neighborhood, there are high levels of poverty all around the perimeter of the school zone, and a surprising number of students really belongs to neither zone—they are homeless. "It's almost as if there are two separate schools within Murray Hill Middle School," Jill says. Unfortunately the children from the wealthy neighborhood make up almost all of the gifted and talented classes.

Jill teaches students from the poverty perimeters, many of whom are struggling readers. She described her students:

> They have not had a strong conversational experience at home, so most of their vocabulary is from what they hear on TV. They don't read at home. Their reading has been mostly out of basals or workbooks to build a skill base, so they think reading is purely decoding. It's very hard to get them to think beyond a literal level.

## VOCABULARY ROUTINES

Jill can't move her students out of the poverty perimeters, but she has a comprehensive literacy plan to move them beyond the learning perimeters. Vocabulary instruction is just one part of that plan. Jill has a number of vocabulary strategies she uses on a regular basis, ideas she has gathered from professional reading, staff development, colleagues, and her own creativity. (See chapter 10 for more on professional growth.)

### Word Splash

For prereading vocabulary development, Jill pulls words from the text to be read and "splashes" them across a piece of butcher paper. The class talks about the words, predicting what they could mean, looking for relationships among the words, and making connections to their background knowledge. As the unit or novel progresses, Jill encourages students to use words from the word splash in conversations and in their writing. This provides a good comprehension check as Jill assesses whether the words are used appropriately.

### Make It Mine Words

Jill's students frequently self-assess their vocabulary knowledge using the knowledge rating chart you read about in chapter 1. Jill lists words from a text students will be reading, and each student individually ranks his/her level of understanding for each word. Not surprisingly, some students mark + (I know it well) for all or nearly all of the words, especially at the beginning of the year, so Jill models the fact that it is OK if they don't know all the words. "Everybody has words at each of these levels," Jill tells the students. Then she gives examples from her own reading or conversations, writing each word on the board with the symbol showing her level of understanding: - + √ *.

One day, for example, Jill explained to her students,

> My sister is a nurse. Sometimes we talk about our jobs. When she uses the word *inoculations*—that's a plus—I know it well. I've had plenty of shots in my life. When she starts talking about *macrobiology*—that's a check—I recognize it in context; it has something to do with biology. If she says *encephalopathy*—dot—I've heard of it, but I don't know what it means. I'm sure if I picked up her nurse's book there would be many words I would have to say, "Minus—I never saw it before." Vocabulary is an individual thing. There are words for every column for every person. It's just that the words are different for different people.

Jill meets with students in small groups or one-on-one to go over their ratings. They pay particular attention to the words students marked as - *I never saw it before* or * *I've heard of it, but I don't know what it means.* Jill calls those words their "make it mine" words. She and the students talk about what they will do to own the words. She reminds them that they can use the dictionary, but they also need other strategies.

> There isn't always a dictionary available when you need it. I teach them how to paraphrase if they do use the dictionary so that I know they really comprehend the meaning of the word. I also tell them it's alright to ask someone. Most people do that.

Sometimes Jill incorporates a mnemonic for the "make it mine words." Students are asked to draw a real-life illustration of the word. For example, the word *lanky* was on one of the lists. A student drew a picture of his tall, thin brother and wrote the caption, "My brother is lanky."

Jill shared the benefits of working with a knowledge rating chart:

> It helps the students become aware of where they are in their vocabulary knowledge. It gives them confidence because of the words they know, and it helps them become aware of what they need. I try to do this only with words that are critical to understanding the text. As with any vocabulary routine, I don't want to overdo it or they will lose interest.

## Vocabulary Tree

Like Joanna Newton (chapter 3), Jill and her students work extensively with Greek and Latin word roots. She introduces the word root, and then students are challenged to collect examples from conversations and print throughout the week for the vocabulary tree bulletin board. The word root is displayed on the roots of the tree, and words the students found, along with their meanings, are displayed on the branches. Jill finds the vocabulary tree serves as a mnemonic to help students remember how Greek and Latin roots work.

## Baby Words

In chapter 4 you read about Jeri Powers's favorite vocabulary strategy, exhausted words map. Jill also employs this strategy on a regular basis; however, she humorously calls it "baby words." When her students repeatedly use those tired (exhausted) words like *said, happy, sad*, Jill tells them, "You learned those words when you were a baby. You're ready for more sophisticated words." It must be noted here that Jill's comments are never offered in a sarcastic manner. She has a great sense of humor, and she conveys it in a playful tone of voice.

The list of "baby words" is not extensive—usually five to ten words for the whole year, depending on the students and their needs. When a "baby word" is heard repeatedly, Jill and the students create a list of synonyms. The students write the "baby word" along with synonyms on a strip of paper, and the words are kept at their desks to be used in writing and conversation.

Eventually Jill hosts a "baby words" party. Students are encouraged to bring in teddy bears, blankets, and pacifiers. They have cookies and milk next to a box decorated as a baby bed. "Now," Jill says teasingly, "throw in your blankies. No more baby words, right?"

## Vocabulary Bookmarks

When students are preparing for a new novel, Jill creates vocabulary bookmarks that they can put in their books and refer to as needed. On one side she lists key vocabulary words, and students predict what the words will mean. The students meet with partners and discuss their predictions. Then the whole class discusses the words.

The reverse side of the bookmark is for individual vocabulary building where students fill in their own words as they are reading. Jill does one-on-one conferences with students to discuss the words they chose. She's prepared for the student who says, "I know all the words." She reads each text ahead of the students and highlights words she thinks the student might not know. When a student claims to know all the words, she points out some of her words, and the student nearly always finds some to add to his/her bookmark.

## JILL JOHNSON-MCMULLAN'S FAVORITE: CONTEXT CLUES

Jill thinks knowing how to use context clues is "the single most important vocabulary skill students can have because it helps them with comprehension." When readers use context, they use passage and sentence meaning as well as their own experiences to predict unknown words.

While some researchers argue that context clues are an unreliable source for figuring out unknown words, Janet Allen (1999) supports the use of context clues with the following argument:

> If average fifth graders spend about twenty-five minutes a day reading, they encounter about twenty thousand unfamiliar words. If one-twentieth of those words can be figured out from context, they learn about a thousand new words per year from that strategy; hardly an insignificant amount! (p. 21)

In its review of vocabulary research, the National Reading Panel (2000) concluded that children use clues in the text to help decipher new words. Moreover, Nagy, Anderson, and Herman (1987) found that between 25 to 50 percent of annual vocabulary growth can be attributed to incidental learning from context.

Jill believes students learn to use context clues best through a gradual release of responsibility (Pearson & Gallagher, 1983). The gradual release of responsibility model incorporates a progression from teacher modeling to shared reading and writing, to guided reading and writing in small groups, to independent reading and writing.

Early in the year Jill reads picture books aloud in order to model how to use context clues to help with an unknown word. She chooses quality children's literature that sixth-grade students will enjoy. For example, recently she read aloud *Mufaro's Beautiful Daughters* (Steptoe, 1987). In preparation for the discussion, Jill looked for words within the text that would probably be new to her students and that contained context clues, picture clues, or both. The words she found included *plot, bountiful, chamber, enclosure, considerate,* and *proclaimed.*

As with the knowledge rating chart, Jill knows not to overdo it. She chose only two words from the list to discuss: *bountiful* and *considerate,* words they will likely encounter in other texts or in conversations. She read the book in its entirety, stopping for predictions along the way but not pointing out the targeted words. After students had adequate time to discuss the book, Jill went back to the pages where the targeted words were found and read them again, in the context of the story.

> Nyasha kept a small plot of land, on which she grew millet, sunflowers, yams, and vegetables. She always sang as she worked, and some said it was her singing that made her crops more bountiful than anyone else's.
> Mufaro knew nothing of how Manyara treated Nyasha, and Nyasha was too considerate of her father's feelings to complain.

Then Jill modeled how she could use text and picture clues to figure out what *bountiful* and *considerate* mean.

After teacher modeling, students practice using context clues as Jill scaffolds. She pulls difficult words from the novels they read in class and gives the words, embedded in a section of text, to the students. She asks them,

> See how these words can get you stuck? If you can't understand the story, then you need to figure out these words. But you can't run to the dictionary every time you meet a new word. That's not realistic. So let's look at this passage and think about what would make sense.

Sometimes the words she chooses are totally new to the students; at other times they are familiar words that have a meaning that is new to the students. For example, when they were reading *The Giver* (Lowry, 2003), Jill targeted the word *release*, a word they knew to mean "to let go." As they discussed what was happening in the text, students began to understand that in the context of this story, *released* meant "killed." As the year goes on students become more and more independent with using context clues.

Jill also embeds new words in the context of conversations. She described how she does that:

> If I know a word is coming that we will need for our reading, I use it a lot before we get to it. For example, if we are going to study bias in an author's writing, I will say, "You are so biased." They ask, "What are you talking about?" It gives them background knowledge to discuss biased writing.
>
> If we are going to discuss character traits, I might use the word *obstinate*. A student will usually pick up on it and say, "You use the word *obstinate* a lot." Then we talk about what they think it means from the context where I used it. By the time we get to the obstinate character, they have a pretty good understanding of the word.

Sometimes Jill chooses words that are not connected to their reading but are chosen to build listening vocabulary. She writes them on the whiteboard or on a piece of paper that she posts in the room. She described what happens:

> It doesn't have to be something they're reading. Sometimes it's a social skill we need to discuss. One year I had a class that was often off-task. I taped the word *irrelevant* above the board. One day Sjuan wasn't paying attention to the lesson. Suddenly he raised his hand and pointed to *irrelevant* and asked, "What does that word mean?" I responded, "Now, number one, I know you weren't paying attention, and number two, *irrelevant* means 'unrelated to the task at hand'— just asking me what *irrelevant* means was irrelevant to what we are discussing right now." We all laughed. I kept the word up all year. When they got off-task, all I had to do was point to *irrelevant*.

## CONCLUSION

Test-prep "skill a week" doesn't work for Jill. "It would be hard to rationalize why I'd do that," she observed. Although she struggles to fit everything in, she does it her way with the strategies above, read alouds, independent reading, and word walls. "What I teach has to be embedded in the text and in the students' individual needs," Jill declared. She has learned that when she focuses on student needs in authentic contexts, vocabulary growth is inevitable.

## REFLECTION AND ACTION

The following questions are designed to help you think through your vocabulary instruction, either alone or with a group of colleagues. The reflection you do is an important part of reading the chapter. The action that results is what puts you among the ranks of great literacy teachers.

1. Research is mixed on the efficacy of using context clues. What do you think? Support your opinion with research or examples from your own classroom.
2. To what extent are you able to "do it your way"? Do state standards, required local curriculum, and high-stakes tests limit "your way"? What are some negotiables and nonnegotiables for your teaching? Use the "carousel" meeting procedure below with your discussion group for this question.
3. Jill Johnson-McMullen gets many of her vocabulary instruction ideas from professional reading, staff development, colleagues, and her own creativity. Talk about where most of your ideas come from. Do you get ideas from each of those sources? If not, could you?
4. Give an example of when you could use a gradual release of responsibility to teach vocabulary.
5. What picture books do you use to teach vocabulary?
6. What is one thing from this chapter that you would like to include in your own classroom?

## MEETING PROCEDURE: CAROUSEL

| | |
|---|---|
| Purpose: | Discussion of important issues |
| Advantage: | All voices are heard |
| | Generates reflective conversation |
| Disadvantage: | Can be time consuming |
| Steps: | |

1. Participants divide into small groups (four or five). Each group has a piece of chart paper.
2. Pose a question or topic. For this discussion, use question 2 from "Reflection and Action."
3. Each group discusses the question and records reactions on chart paper.
4. Tape the papers on the wall around the room.

5. Each group goes from chart to chart, reading what other groups wrote and writing comments/questions.
6. Each group revisits its own chart to see what others wrote.
7. Debrief as a large group. What similarities did you see on the charts? Were there things your group had not thought about? What did you learn?

Adapted from ReadWriteThink: "Brainstorming and Reviewing Using the Carousel Strategy" www.readwritethink.org/professional-development /strategy-guides/brainstorming-reviewing-using-carousel-30630.html.

## Chapter Seven

# Teacher Modeling
# for Vocabulary Instruction

In his book *Joining the Literacy Club*, Frank Smith (1987) talks about the social nature of literacy learning. Smith maintains that children want to be like the significant people in their lives. For children, most often those people are their teachers and parents. When they see adults they depend upon admire reading and writing, they want to join the metaphorical "literacy club."

Effective vocabulary teachers invite their students to join the *word-lovers chapter* of the *literacy club*. They use sophisticated words in conversations with their students, point out interesting words as they read to students, and help students make good word choices in their writing.

What awesome words have you heard this week? (See chapter 5 for more on "awesome words.") Pay attention to words you hear in the media or in conversations, words you read in a book, words you read on a food package, and so on. Tell your students where you found the words and what they mean. Teacher modeling is an essential component of vocabulary instruction.

## A LIFE OF READING, WRITING,
## AND THINKING IN KENT, OHIO

For Michele McCombs, teacher modeling comes naturally. "I live my life as a reader, and a writer, and a thinker," she said. "The key is how to transfer that to my teaching. It is seamless for me. When I teach, I'm modeling how I live my own life." Michele described what her life as a reader looks like.

When I read something I always write in the margins. I like my own books because I like to underline, circle, and make lists. I flip to the inside cover and write interesting words I just love and want to use in my own writing. Right now I am reading *Mennonite in a Little Black Dress* (Janzen, 2010). I've never read a book with such a plethora of vocabulary. I'm making a list in the back. You just have to read it!

Reading and writing are core aspects of Michele's identity, and she can't help but share that with anyone who will listen, especially her students. Her enthusiasm is contagious. Her modeling is effective. And her students are learning what a life of reading, writing, and thinking looks like.

Michele teaches second grade at Longcoy Elementary School in Kent, Ohio, where the student population is very diverse. About 50 percent of students receive free and reduced lunch; however, there is also a large population of students from professional homes because the school sits in the shadow of a major university where some of their parents teach. Michele describes her school: "The diversity of the community is reflected in the diversity of our students' needs. Some are significantly above reading level and some are significantly below. It's a real challenge to meet each child where their needs are."

## ASSESSING STUDENTS' INTERESTS AND NEEDS

Michele begins assessing her students on the first day of school. The class has quiet reading time while she conferences with individual students. She likens reading conferences to a book club. She tells them that she wants to find out what they are good at and what their reading interests are. "Once I find out about your interests, then I can go to the library and pick out a few books just for you! If I could get any book you wanted, what would it be?"

In addition to having an informal conversation about their interests, Michele completes a running record for each child. She asks each child to read orally from a district-adopted text or a book from her own library, such as the *Henry and Mudge* books by Cynthia Rylant, *Horrible Harry* books by Suzy Kline and Frank Remkiewicz, or *Junie B. Jones* books by Barbara Park and Denise Brunkus.

She finds these books especially suitable for conducting running records with students because they are popular with children and written at an instructional reading level (95–97 percent word recognition and 75–89 percent comprehension) for many second-grade students. If she sees that the text is at a frustration level (less than 90 percent word recognition and less than 50 percent comprehension) she immediately chooses a different book. If a text seems to be too easy, she reaches for a higher-level text.

The running record includes any miscues or self-corrections the child makes so that Michele can analyze whether the child was using information from the meaning of the text (semantics), the structure of the sentence (syntax), or visual cues (grapho-phonics). Each student also does a retelling of the text.

For each running record Michele completes a two-column sheet. On the right side she makes notes about miscues, self-corrections, and the retelling. On the left side she notes vocabulary words encountered in the text that are interesting or that the student does not know. One day, for example, Laurel read a short text about hurricanes. She knew the word *eye*, but she did not know its meaning in this context so Michele made a note so that she and Laurel could return to it later.

By the end of the first full week of school Michele has a folder for each child. She explained what she does with what she has learned:

> Right away I go to the library with my class list. Next to each name I have brief notes about interests and reading level. This is a quick way to match books to each reader. I say to Jacob, "Here's a book on horses. I hope you like it because I know you love horses." Last year Jordan was so into princesses, so I got lots of princess books for her. I said, "Here, Jordan. I think you will like these. If anyone else is interested, there are enough princess books for all of you." As the year goes on, students start looking for books for each other. If someone finds a princess book or a fairy book they bring it in for Jordan.

Michele continues to add to each child's folder as she assesses students one-on-one throughout the year. As she gets to know students, she chooses books she knows each will like for the reading conferences. Sometimes students choose which books they want to bring to the conference.

Michele revisits the folders often to see what vocabulary words need to be reinforced for individual students. "How do you know when a child knows the word?" Michele pondered. "Often I can tell when he does a retelling or talks about a book. If he uses the word appropriately, that's a strong clue." In addition to guiding instruction, the reading conference folders provide concrete documentation for school intervention team meetings.

## VOCABULARY ROUTINES

### Quiet Reading

In order to support their vocabulary growth, Michele's students have quiet reading time at least once a day, twice on most days. There are many quiet spaces in the room with books in carpeted areas. In order to help the children learn the expectations of quiet reading time, each year Michele gathers eight-by-ten photographs of students during reading, writing, or conferencing times. She laminates them and put magnets on the back so they stick easily to the chalkboard. The photos serve as models for what is expected. Michele explains how effective the photos are: "The kids can see the focus and concentration on the faces of my former students. All I have to say is, 'Please, look like DeEvann,' if someone is off track. This has worked very well."

## Read Alouds

Michele reads aloud to her class three times a day. At the beginning of the morning, read aloud, which is usually a picture book, sets the tone for the day. She usually chooses a book that will reinforce a language arts concept the students are working on such as making inferences. After lunch recess, the read aloud is usually a chapter book, such as one from the *Horrible Harry* series by Suzy Kline and Frank Remkiewicz or *The Stories Julian Tells* series by Ann Cameron and Ann Strugnell. In the afternoon Michele reads a book, usually a picture book, related to a social studies or science unit of study. She may read the entire book or just parts of it.

Michele explained why she finds this time to be invaluable for building vocabulary:

> We just come across great words. One day I was reading *Mercy Watson Goes for a Ride* (DiCamillo & VanDusen, 2009) and we came across the phrase *porcine wonder. Porcine.* "You, my dear, are a porcine wonder. But even porcine wonders cannot drive cars" (p. 4). I didn't even know how to pronounce it. I printed it on the board, and we talked about how we might pronounce it and what it might mean. Then we looked it up in the dictionary. We learned the marks on how to pronounce it and what it means. It means "relating to a pig." Then we had to discuss that. What does "relating to a pig" mean? You have to be careful though. These discussions need to happen selectively. You don't want to overanalyze literature. Just do it as it comes up naturally.

## Patriotic Songs and Texts

Michele uses patriotic songs and texts like the Pledge of Allegiance to teach second-grade state standards for government, which include recognition of U.S. symbols, monuments, and memorials. The songs and texts are rich with vocabulary that is new for most second-grade students. Michele observed,

> Even a familiar song like "My Country 'Tis of Thee" has lots of words we can discuss. Just look at the title. What does *'tis* and *thee* mean? Sometimes I give them the full text and they circle the words they don't know. Then we talk about how they could find out what the words mean—ask someone, use a dictionary,

go to the Internet, use context clues. Once they've figured out what the words mean, they write definitions in their own words or draw pictures in the margin beside the words.

"The Star-Spangled Banner" is full of rich vocabulary—*ramparts, hailed, twilight, gleaming, broad, gallantly.* They put these songs into their poetry notebooks. Again, you have to be careful not to overdo it, but I find the students really are interested in knowing what the words mean.

Michele typically spends about two weeks on the Pledge of Allegiance, doing two lines a day. Students fold a sheet of paper in half lengthwise. On the left side they write the vocabulary words. On the right side they write a definition or draw a picture to illustrate its meaning. (See Figure 7.1) "We start by talking about *United States.* What is *United States*? It's a country. Well, what does *country* mean?" The opportunities are nearly endless with such texts.

Michele's students are encouraged to use their newly acquired words in conversation and in their own writing. Often the words show up in poems they write for their poetry notebooks. "We inspire each other to write poetry and model our work after that of the poets we study," Michele noted proudly.

## Connecting Spelling and Vocabulary Instruction

Michele pondered, "How do you talk about vocabulary without talking about spelling? They are like brother and sister. We do a lot with Greek and Latin roots, and prefixes and suffixes in our spelling lessons." Michele groups her students into four spelling levels according to her knowledge of spelling stages. The groups are flexible and fluid. She takes the base list from their spelling book and builds on it to develop spelling lists that move students from basic spelling to a knowledge of how words work.

For example, one week Michele discussed the word root *pedi* (feet) with her students. All students were involved in the discussion of the word root and various words that include the root, but each group had a related spelling word that was appropriate for his/her spelling level. (See chapter 3 for more on word roots.)

The week's lists included the following:

List A: pedal
List B: pedal
List C: centipede
List D: pedicure

The Pledge of Allegiance

| | |
|---|---|
| I pledge allegiance | I promise |
| to the flag | to the Flag |
| of the United States of America | of the U.SA. |
| and to the republic | and to the government |
| for which it stands | for which it is a symbol |
| one nation | one country |
| under God | Under God |
| indivisible | which cannot be spilt up |
| with liberty and justice | whith freedom and faihness |
| for all. | for everyone. |

**Figure 7.1.   Pledge of Alligiance Vocabulary Study**

The next week they studied the word root *man* (hand). The spelling lists were:

List A: hand
List B: manual
List C: manual
List D: manicure

Michele also structures spelling lists around common spelling patterns. She cited the following story as evidence that the spelling-vocabulary connection is working:

Early on in one year we worked with the spelling pattern *tion*. The kids just took off with finding those words. During quiet reading time they would write *tion* words on a sticky note and bring them to me. Sometimes they would bring them from home. We were using so many sticky notes I told them they had to fill up the entire sticky before they brought it to me. I stuck them on chart paper, and then we would discuss them. Finally we had so many we couldn't always share all of them, but I promised I would read all of them.

This went on the entire year. I saved all the sticky notes, and I had this humongous stack of yellow stickies. David was the most excited. He would bring words from home. How could a teacher not get excited?

Education
Vacation
Nashtion
Salvation
Plantation
Oporation
relation
celobration

**Figure 7.2. David's *tion* Word List**

David Smith

## MICHELE MCCOMBS'S FAVORITE:
## INDEX CARD CONVERSATIONS

Although it's difficult for Michele to pick one favorite vocabulary strategy, she really enjoys "index card conversations." She chooses vocabulary words from a story the children have just read, puts them on index cards, and places them facedown in the center of each table group. Students take turns drawing two cards and using them both in a sentence that tells something about the story.

For example, when Michele pulled words from the series *Mr. Putter and Tabby* by Cynthia Rylant and John McDonough, one student drew cards with the words *rescue* and *Mr. Putter*. The student shared the sentence, "Mr. Putter rescued Tabby from the animal shelter because she was an old cat and Mr. Putter is an old person." The activity often becomes a form of retelling, and Michele can listen for both comprehension and vocabulary acquisition. "It's fun because it's a conversation about books," she shared.

## CONCLUSION

Michele summed up her vocabulary instruction by saying, "It's model, model, model. When I'm reading something I share it with my students. I say, 'Listen to this. I love the way the author describes this place. I'm going to put it in my writer's notebook.'" Michele believes teachers have to live a reader's and writer's life. She poignantly asked, "I model my life as a reader and writer. If a teacher doesn't have that life, how can she do her important work well with students?"

## REFLECTION AND ACTION

The following questions are designed to help you think through your vocabulary instruction, either alone or with a group of colleagues. The reflection you do is an important part of reading the chapter. The action that results is what puts you among the ranks of great literacy teachers.

1. Michele McCombs likes to make notes of interesting words as she is reading. This week as you are reading a text of your choice (book, magazine, newspaper, etc.) make a list of interesting words you encounter. Share them with your colleagues. Is this something you would do on a regular basis? Why or why not?

2. Do you teach patriotic songs and/or the Pledge of Allegiance to your students? Look through the words in the texts and highlight any that could build vocabulary for your students. Ask the people in your discussion group to share the words they found and how they plan to teach the meanings of those words.
3. Do you connect vocabulary instruction with spelling? If so, how do you do that? If not, can you think of ways to begin making that connection?
4. Describe your reader's and writer's life. Is there anything you would like to change about that life? What concrete steps could you take to get started?
5. What is one thing from this chapter that you would like to include in your own classroom?

*Chapter Eight*

# Filling Your Classroom with Words

Have you ever been around a young child as she learned to talk? It seems magical. One day she's babbling and you can't understand her, and then before long she's saying sentences that surprise you and make you laugh. How did she learn to talk like that? In chapter 1 you learned that the "magic" actually lies in the way parents talk to their children, and the lack of parent-child conversations can result in a 30-million-word gap (Hart & Risley, 2003).

The "magic" applies to your vocabulary instruction just as it does to young children learning to talk. If you want your students to increase their vocabularies, you must fill your classroom with words, both oral and written. (See chapter 12 for more on oral vocabulary support in the classroom.)

Many teachers use word walls as a way to immerse students in written vocabulary. A word wall is a bulletin board or section of the classroom wall that contains a collection of words, usually in alphabetical order and written with thick black marker or with large letters on colored paper. The wall might contain sight words, content area words, words from books students are reading, or other words that are relevant to the class at that time.

Word walls first became popular in the 1990s. Today it is rare to walk into an elementary classroom that does not have a word wall, and in the past few years word walls have become increasingly popular in middle school and high school reading classes as well as in content area classes.

## A WORD-FILLED CLASSROOM IN ORLANDO, FLORIDA

Every wall in Patrick Hernan's first-grade classroom is a word wall. Certainly Patrick has the traditional word wall with high-frequency words his students use for reading and writing, but that wall is only a small sampling of how Patrick fills his classroom with words. One wall holds chart papers filled with words that contain long and short vowels. There are also charts with words illustrating common digraphs and blends, charts with word families, and charts with rhyming words.

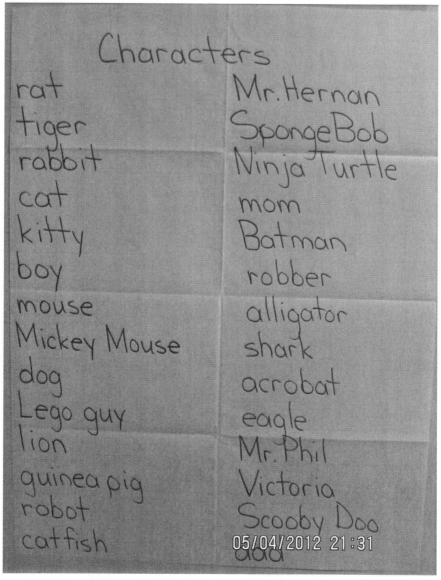

**Figure 8.1.  Characters Wall Chart**

On another wall you will see charts with nouns and verbs, charts with number words, and charts with transition words (e.g., *through, however, also*). There are charts with lists to remind students of story elements (characters, settings—places and time—and feelings). One chart points out that Mr. Hernan, a shark, and an acrobat could be characters in a story (see figure 8.1).

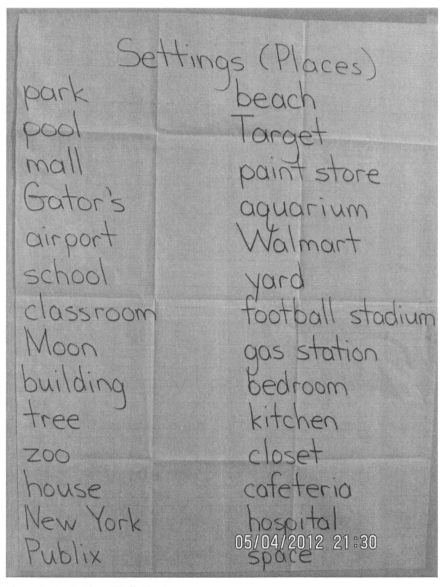

Figure 8.2. Settings Wall Chart

Another chart reminds students that the setting might include a place (e.g., beach, gas station, classroom) or time (e.g., afternoon, sunset, birthday, center time). (See figures 8.2 and 8.3.)

Still another chart highlights words to express feelings (e.g., *scared, proud, upset, weird*). (See figure 8.4.)

There is a daily message on chart paper and a weather chart. One wall chart displays color words, and another shows months and days of the week. One corner in the room hosts a pocket chart with words related to the week's language arts lesson. The chalkboard lists learning goals, essential questions, and exit activities for every subject. And the best part of all these displays is that nearly all the words were generated through discussions with the students.

## Word Wall Routine

Like the other teachers in this book, Patrick understands the importance of routines in developing independent learners. (See chapter 2 for more on the

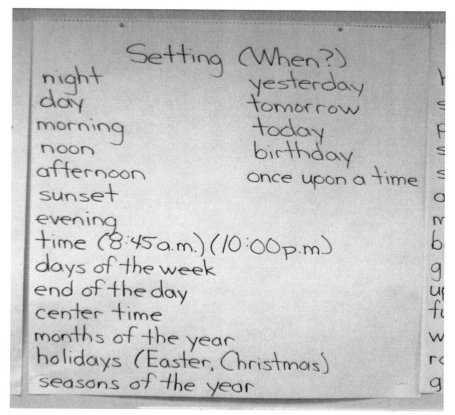

**Figure 8.3. Settings (Time) Wall Chart**

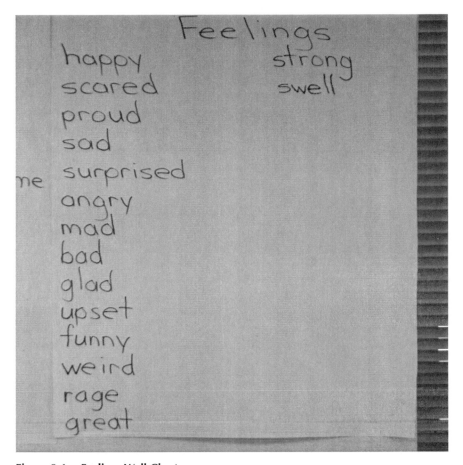

**Figure 8.4. Feelings Wall Chart**

importance of routines.) His routine for the traditional word wall involves a five-day sequence of activities that includes vocabulary development as well as sight word recognition.

Monday: Students chorally read words on the word wall. Then Patrick tells students, "Here are our *friends* for this week," and proceeds to introduce several new words. (Patrick explained, "Calling them *friends* makes the learning personal. It helps the students connect with the words.") The words are added alphabetically to the word wall.

| Tuesday | Students review the word wall once again, with a special focus on their new *friends*. Patrick uses this opportunity to extend sight word recognition into vocabulary development. Sometimes students think of synonyms or antonyms for the new words. In a recent lesson, students discussed different meanings of the word *right* and explored the homophones *through* and *threw*. After this vocabulary development, students apply what they have learned by using the words in their own writing. |

| Wednesday: | On this day Patrick reads a story that is related to phonics skills students are learning that week. The stories are carefully chosen to reinforce the phonics concept while at the same time building vocabulary. For example, recently the students were learning the sound of /fl/, so Patrick read aloud a story about a flamingo. Being Florida residents, the word *flamingo* was not new to the students, but the story also contained the words *flock* and *flustered*, so Patrick led a discussion on the meanings of these words. |

Patrick asked, "When you are doing a puzzle and the pieces don't fit, how do you feel?"

Gavin replied, "Angry."

Brooke added, "Aggravated."

Patrick said, "Yes. When you're aggravated or angry you are feeling flustered. That's how the flamingo felt when she couldn't fly. She was flustered."

| Thursday: | After reviewing the new words and their meanings, students are given sentences with words missing, and they must use context clues to decide which words go in the blanks. (See chapter 6 for more on context clues.) |

| Friday: | The class plays word wall bingo. |

## PATRICK HERNAN'S FAVORITE: WORD WALL BINGO

When asked, "What is the most popular game in Mr. Hernan's class?" students shout in unison, "Word wall bingo!" Patrick's students look forward to Fridays, not because it's almost the weekend but because they get to play their favorite word game. It is by far the most popular activity of the week. Each student is given two blank bingo cards. Students choose which words from the word wall they will write on their own cards so that each child's card is different. Patrick begins by playing the theme song from a popular TV game show. The children excitedly hum along as they prepare for the first word to be called and used in a sentence. Often students can be heard echoing the sentence, thus providing themselves and their classmates with aural reinforcement.

When Patrick talks about word wall bingo he's nearly as animated as the students. He shared,

> A few years ago I had a very low student who was to be retained in first grade. He was lacking in vocabulary because the family support was lacking, he was younger than most of the students, and he had recently moved from another state. And then one day he did it! He recognized ten words and yelled, "Bingo!" Finally he had connected. He had the understanding of what those words meant. It was a turning point. To see him win that day . . . to see the lightbulb go off. . . to see he knew those words . . . By the end of the year there was so much more confidence in him.

## CONCLUSION

In Patrick Hernan's classroom, children's eyes are constantly coming to rest on words. Throughout the day, children's ears are constantly hearing new words. Throughout the week, children's voices are constantly using new words. Throughout the year, children's brains are constantly building vocabulary. Classrooms like Patrick Hernan's bring the magic into vocabulary acquisition.

## REFLECTION AND ACTION

The following questions are designed to help you think through your vocabulary instruction, either alone or with a group of colleagues. The reflection you do is an important part of reading the chapter. The action that results is what puts you among the ranks of great literacy teachers.

1. What are some ways you fill your classroom with words?
2. How do you decide which words will be displayed in your classroom?
3. Do you have a routine for your word wall? If so, describe it to your discussion group. If not, think of routine possibilities.
4. Describe some activities for using word walls to enhance vocabulary development.
5. What is one thing from this chapter that you would like to include in your own classroom?

## Chapter Nine

# Teaching Vocabulary
# in Meaningful Contexts

No doubt your memory of vocabulary instruction when you were a student is like that of millions of other Americans. Do you remember being assigned lists of words to learn? How often did the words seem randomly chosen—disconnected from anything you were reading at the time? Did you have to visit the dictionary, write the definitions, and use the words in sentences? Did you have a Friday test over the words? And, most importantly, did you remember any of the words a week later?

Such assignments are not effective for at least three reasons. First, cognitive science has shown that human beings best learn those things that have meaning for them. For most students, learning vocabulary words in isolation makes it difficult to make connections with background knowledge, personal experiences, or what they are learning in other subjects.

Second, finding definitions in the dictionary does not assure understanding. Years ago my son was in middle school and given such an assignment. One of the words was *remnant*, for which he found the definition: "something left over." He proceeded to write his sentence: "We are having remnants for dinner."

Finally, this method of vocabulary instruction is not effective because it is not fun. "It is drudgery, and students treat it as such. The unfortunate consequence is that students may learn that any type of word exploration is boring and to be avoided" (Rasinski, Padak, & Fawcett, 2010, p. 142). Successful vocabulary instruction situates new words within meaningful contexts.

# LEARNING VOCABULARY THROUGH SUPPLEMENTAL READING INSTRUCTION IN GANADO, ARIZONA

Elaina Vann teaches in Ganado, Arizona, on a Native American Indian reservation. Ninety-two percent of Ganado Primary School students are Navajo. The free and reduced lunch count is approximately 80 percent. Elaina loops with her students over four years. They enter her classroom as kindergartners and stay with her through first, second, and third grades. When this chapter was written, she was beginning her fifth set of looped students.

When asked to describe her successful vocabulary instruction, Elaina responded, "I don't do anything magical." She continued with a little laugh, "I'm a different kind of teacher. I'm the type that bucks the system." Even so, Elaina dutifully teaches her district-adopted reading text; however, she has also developed her own supplemental reading program, which focuses on literature study. The vocabulary words her students learn do not come from a random list; they come from the literature students are reading.

Sometimes Elaina runs into former students who are now in middle school or high school, and she finds they are keeping up with literature. They chat about authors or ask Elaina if she has read certain books. Graduates come back regularly to talk with her. One student recently told her, "You really helped me through college because you pushed reading. I love reading so much. When my friends would say, 'Let's go out,' I would answer, 'No. I need to read.'" While Elaina may think what she does is not magical, these students would surely disagree. For them her reading instruction was magical.

## Vocabulary Study with Literature

The seed for Elaina's supplemental reading instruction was planted when she was in college. She described what happened:

> We were given a list of books we should have read in order to be prepared for college. The other students were pointing out all the books they had read from the list. I felt really inadequate. I felt like I wasn't prepared for college. As a teacher, I thought about that. Why would I want to do that to a student? I decided I should share classic literature with my students. They need to know "The Three Little Pigs" and "Little Red Riding Hood." They need to be familiar with classic works so that no matter where in the world they go, they have that basis.

Elaina claimed, "I really don't teach vocabulary. I teach reading. Reading and conversations—those are the main ways kids learn words in my class." Although she doesn't plan specific vocabulary lessons, the way she embeds vocabulary into literature study assures that her students are connecting with the words—getting meaning.

Over the four years that Elaina's students are with her, they are introduced to traditional stories as well as to well-known children's authors. Beginning in kindergarten, she sets the stage for the ongoing literature study by reading aloud from authors like Eric Carle, Dr. Seuss, Ezra Jack Keats, and P. D. Eastman. As they move into first, second, and third grades, the students study books by these same well-known authors but in an increasingly complex manner.

For example, first graders find all of Eric Carle's books and look for similarities and differences among them. They discover that Carle's books involve animals. In second grade they learn to analyze the characters and settings of familiar books. Among other things, they see that Keats always has a small child as a main character. By third grade they are looking for themes in the familiar books. Elaina elaborated,

> We don't read a book one time and then leave it. I tell the students they should never read a book just one time. We reread it in a week, maybe a month later, and in future years. Their vocabulary develops from those books because they hear it, read it, and use it many times.

While they are revisiting familiar books, Elaina continually adds more quality books to their literature study. By third grade students are reading classics like *Charlotte's Web* (White, 2001), *Island of the Blue Dolphins* (O'Dell, 1987), and *A Single Shard* (Park, 2003) as well as informational texts like the *Magic Tree House* series by Mary Pope Osborne. "I choose books that allow students to ask questions and play with language," she says.

Elaina's students acquire increasingly sophisticated vocabulary through their interaction with the books in literature study. Elaina explained,

> The most important thing is that I try to give it all meaning. When I used to give them a vocabulary list and do the textbook vocabulary activities it just didn't have meaning for them; they just weren't making connections. Now, with literature study, I don't start with a word list. I start with comprehension and ask what words they need to comprehend the piece. When we read *The Very Hungry Caterpillar* (Carle, 1987) in kindergarten, they need to understand what a cocoon is, so we talk about that.
>
> A few days ago we read *The Napping House* (Wood, 1991). We talked about how *dozing*, *napping*, and *sleeping* are all words we can use to talk about the way people sleep. I pull words from the literature study books that are specific to an environment. For example, when second graders read *Charlotte's Web* (White, 2001) we talk about words like *scavenger*, *trough*, and *barn*. Although

we live in a rural area and there are lots of horses, the word *trough* is new to them.

We talk about the kind of language Junie B. Jones (Barbara Park's series) uses and how the language of expository text is different from fiction. In this way the vocabulary makes sense to them.

## Knowledge Boxes

Elaina's students keep vocabulary words they are currently learning in a "knowledge box." Students make their boxes together in class (see figure

**Knowledge Box**

You will create a knowledge box for your vocabulary word cards. (Sometimes families have a special box that they keep their most precious possessions in. These possessions have special meaning attached to them and are often handed down through the family or have a story about them.)

Directions:

Need 2 - 8 ½ x 11" heavy card stock paper.

On one paper decorate the top of your box (draw a design or color with some pattern). You will need to include your name imbedded into the decoration or design on the top of the box. You will also need to include a lock in the design of your cover (lid).

The second sheet of paper is the bottom half of the knowledge box. Measure ¼ of an inch around the edge of the top and one side. Cut ¼ of an edge off of the top and side. Remember this is the bottom of your box. Laminate both pieces with the teacher.

You will fold both pieces into a box. (separately) Bottom piece then top piece.

Fold the paper in half, length wise.

Open it back up and fold one edge (length side) of the paper into the middle fold of the paper.

Fold the other edge of the paper into the middle of the paper.

Keep it folded. Then at each corner, fold the corner to the middle fold line to make a triangle. Fold all four corners.

Keep the diamond shape at the top and bottom and fold over to make a crease (fold) at the base of the triangles.

Place flat and pull open and pop up into a box. Place tape on the ends to keep stable.

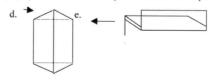

**Figure 9.1.   Knowledge Box**

9.1). Throughout the year they illustrate word cards from books they are reading and place the cards in their knowledge boxes (see figure 9.2).Students visit the boxes when they need to review a word's meaning. They also take their boxes home to share the new words with their families.

### Racing the Sun by Paul Pitts: Chapter 1

### Knowledge Cards

On the back of the vocabulary word card: draw a picture (non-linguistic rendition), or create a sentence that will help you better understand the word. You may also include a picture from the internet or one you created yourself. On the blank cards write words that you would like to use for increasing your understanding. Keep the cards in your knowledge box.

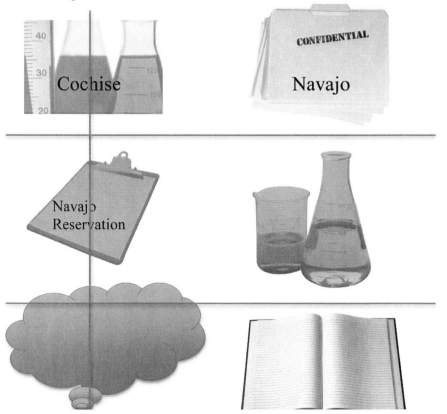

Figure 9.2.   Knowledge Cards

## Vocabulary Study with Nonfiction Texts

Elaina observed, "I found out a long time ago that schoolwide our students scored very low in expository reading on standardized tests. The middle school was telling us that, too." She made some visits to the middle school to observe students in content area classes. "They didn't know how to read a science book," she found. "They were looking for a story line."

Elaina went back to Ganado Elementary School and reviewed the computerized reading program they were using. Students go to the school reading lab daily to take a test on the computer and then check out books that match their corresponding skill level. She looked at the books students were checking out and found the lab had very few nonfiction books. To compound the problem, teachers were using their district-adopted anthologies exclusively, and those contained very few nonfiction texts.

Elaina tried more nonfiction with her students and found they often didn't remember what they had read. "The vocabulary was so new to them," she said.

> I had to start pulling vocabulary out just like I did for our literature studies. Again, I found the words were best learned in context. They had to see how it fits within the world. Right away I noticed a change.

Now Elaina regularly sends students on a nonfiction book hunt (see textbox 9.1). The activity provides a context for discussions about new words the students encounter during their hunt.

## ELAINA VANN'S FAVORITE: VOCABULARY DEVELOPMENT THROUGH THE SENSES

Much of the vocabulary work Elaina plans for students is focused on developing the whole child. She believes learning is best when students' senses are engaged. She attempts to have them touch, see, taste, hear, and feel the words they are learning. Often they create concrete representations of new words with clay or cardboard.

When third graders recently read *A Single Shard* (Park, 2003), they learned the word *pottery*, a term new to many of them. Elaina wanted to take them to a pottery studio in a nearby town, but the school's budget restrictions prohibited that. So in order to reinforce their memory of the word, Elaina had the students make pots from mud they dug. As they discussed how the story's character was so poor he boiled chicken bones and ate the marrow, Elaina

---

**Textbox 9.1.   Nonfiction Book Hunt**

Name _____ Date _____

Hunt and find one book that is about only one of the topics listed below.

Write the title, the author, the main topic, and 3 details about the topic. Write about one detail you didn't know before and one detail you found interesting.

Be ready to share with the classroom. If you need to draw a picture to help you remember, include a sketch.

1. Find a book that is about a weather element.

2. Find a book that is about a historic event (history).

3. Find a book that is about outer space.

4. Find a book that presents something about plants.

5. Find a book that presents an athlete or movie star (biography).

6. Find a book that is about an animal.

---

brought in chicken bones, and you can guess what they did—boiled the bones and ate the marrow.

In order to get a sense of the *trash heaps* where characters in the story often found their meals, Elaina took her students to the school dumpster. They looked, and they smelled. Then she said, "Now, dig through this to find your lunch." Of course they didn't really do it, but it is not likely any student will forget the word *dumpster* or the phrase *trash heap*!

When reading *Island of the Blue Dolphins* (O'Dell, 1987), third graders encountered the word *sorrow*. First they discussed the meaning of the word and what would make someone feel sorrow. Then Elaina had them demonstrate a look of sorrow on their own faces. Sometimes students draw pictures to illustrate feelings or a dramatic event from a story, thus engaging the sense of touch and vision.

Elaina sums up the sensory vocabulary experiences in this way: "In order to get a sense of what someone in the story has gone through, it has to connect to the senses. They have to experience it."

## PARENT INVOLVEMENT

Elaina has noticed recently that some of her kindergartners are beginning school with increasingly limited language skills. "They are not fluent in Navajo, but they also don't have an English base," she explained. "These children aren't getting involved in conversations. They are playing video games and watching TV. They are receiving language, but they don't know how to give it back." Elaina believes parent involvement can make a big difference in children's vocabulary development as they are engaged in literature study.

At the beginning of the year Elaina sends a survey to parents asking about their family's reading habits (see textbox 9.2). Often blank surveys are returned. At parent conferences Elaina says, "I'm sorry. You probably didn't have time to fill this out." Then she begins to ask the survey questions.

---

### Texbox 9.2.   Family Reading Survey

Welcome to Our Class,

Thank you for giving me the opportunity to teach your child this year. We'll be traveling around the world visiting many people and places through our reading. Before we begin our trip, I need a little bit of background information from you.

Parent Literature Survey

1. Please list the type of reading material you have in your house.

2. What is the title of your favorite book?

3. How many minutes a day/night do you spend reading material yourself?

4. How many times through the week do you read the newspaper? Which newspaper do you prefer?

5. What do you like about magazines? Which magazine do you read?

6. What is your child's favorite book?

7. Who is your child's favorite book character?

8. How many minutes a night do you spend reading with your child?

---

Sometimes parents say, "Books are too expensive." With Elaina there are no excuses. She offers books from her classroom.

Elaina sets high expectations for parents and students at the beginning of the year. "I tell them, 'Your child *will* be reading, and you will read two books each night to your child.' They have to do this in order for the child to be in my class. Years ago I started this, and my principal is supportive."

Elaina realizes, "I must try to teach parents as I am teaching their child." She hosts parents nights throughout the school year when she tells parents where their children should be reading compared to national norms. Sometimes parents subsequently ask for worksheets. "I tell them, 'Read two books each night. Here is language. Here is where you're helping your child.'"

A few years ago Elaina established a partnership with a bookstore in the nearest town, more than an hour's drive from the reservation. When parents first began taking their children to the bookstore, the employees were amazed. The students and their parents had no concept of buying books; they treated the store like a library. Eventually they began purchasing books.

Most parents are responsive to Elaina's requests because she has a reputation in the district of being a great literacy teacher. However, "if it doesn't happen in the home, I am dogging parents," she said. "We meet and come up with a plan." If all else fails, Elaina assigns an older student or teacher's assistant to read to the child. Elaina explained, "With parents being involved in reading to their children, the students' language really changes—it matures."

## CONCLUSION

The result of students' vocabulary development through their literature and nonfiction studies is effective. "They learn the same words," Elaina said. "They still learn *continent, weather, cricket,* and *clippity clop,* but when they start with texts, their reading behavior is different." Perhaps it's the closest thing to magical!

## REFLECTION AND ACTION

The following questions are designed to help you think through your vocabulary instruction, either alone or with a group of colleagues. The reflection you do is an important part of reading the chapter. The action that results is what puts you among the ranks of great literacy teachers.

1. What do you think of Elaina Vann's statement, "I really don't teach vocabulary; I teach reading"?

2. Do you agree with Elaina Vann that children should be familiar with literary classics? Why or why not?
3. Teachers frequently say that today's children do not know nursery rhymes or children's stories, such as "Little Red Riding Hood" or "The Three Little Pigs." Do you agree? If so, what is your evidence? What do you think led to the demise of these childhood classics?
4. What percent of texts available in your school library is nonfiction? Gather data about which books students check out most. What percent of classroom reading texts is nonfiction? Is there a need for staff development regarding nonfiction texts in your school?
5. What is one thing from this chapter that you would like to include in your own classroom?

## MEETING PROCEDURE: JIGSAW

| Purpose: | Examine various sides of an issue |
|---|---|
| Advantages: | More information can be shared in a shorter period of time |
| | Participants can focus more deeply on one aspect of an issue rather than dividing their attention among many aspects |
| Disadvantage: | Participants do not get an in-depth understanding of all sides of an issue |

Steps:

1. Participants divide into small groups (four or five). Each group has one part of the topic to discuss in depth. For example, an article or book might be divided into sections with each group having one section to study. For this activity, use questions 1–5 from "Reflection and Action."
2. Each group studies/discusses its assigned part.
3. Each group shares its part with the larger group.

## Chapter Ten

# Professional Development and Vocabulary Instruction

Educational author and staff developer Roland Barth asks us to consider the common instructions given by flight attendants to airline passengers: "In the unlikely event of a drop in cabin pressure, an oxygen mask will drop from an overhead compartment." Then this important directive—"Those of you traveling with small children should first place the mask on your own face and *then*, and only then, place the mask on your child's face." Why? Because you can't help someone else if you are dead!

Barth uses this example as an analogy for teacher learning. He observes, "A school is not different than a 757; if we want youngsters to put on the oxygen mask of learning, we adults must do it first, and right alongside them" (Barth, 2001, p. 25).

There are many venues for professional learning. In chapter 4 Jeri Powers stressed the importance of professional reading. In chapter 5 Jackie Zaucha espoused the value of networking with colleagues. Many teachers pursue advanced degrees at the university level. Other teachers attend professional development conferences and workshops. Some teachers pursue one or more of those venues. Some do it all.

No one way is best. Each teacher must decide for himself or herself what is needed to learn and grow. But the key word in that previous sentence is *must*. Each teacher *must* decide what is needed to learn and grow, because children can't learn from teachers who are learning-dead themselves.

## PROFESSIONAL DEVELOPMENT
## IN CHULA VISTA, CALIFORNIA

For several years there has been a huge push in California for teaching academic vocabulary to meet the needs of the large English language learner

89

(ELL) population. Universities and school districts work together to provide ongoing professional development to help teachers meet the vocabulary needs of their students.

Susan Dowell teaches a fourth- and fifth-grade combination class at Myrtle S. Finney Elementary School, which is near the border in Chula Vista, California. Finney is a Title I school with a predominantly Hispanic population (74 percent). Fifty-one percent of the students are ELLs. The majority of Susan's students have had limited exposure to words they will encounter in grade-level literature and content area reading. Consequently, these students struggle with reading and writing.

Susan exemplifies professional learning. She earned a master of arts in education/reading at San Diego State University. She is a member of the International Reading Association and reads *The Reading Teacher* from cover to cover each month. Her professional reading is extensive, and she loves finding instructional ideas for the upper-elementary-grade classroom. She has also attended extensive professional development sessions that help her teach ELLs.

One of the most valuable professional development sessions Susan has attended is a California Department of Education "best practices" program called Project GLAD (Guided Language Acquisition Design). The program focuses on language acquisition, academic language, and literacy with a strong emphasis on vocabulary development. Many of Susan's vocabulary routines have resulted from her GLAD training.

## VOCABULARY ROUTINES

### Think Alouds

Think aloud is a strategy wherein a person verbalizes what she or he is thinking. Classroom think alouds allow teachers and students to explain the mental processes they use when dealing with an academic task. Susan frequently does think alouds to model how she uses context clues to figure out unknown words. (See chapter 6 for more on context clues.) Her think alouds teach students to monitor their thinking as they encounter unknown words.

Recently Susan did a think aloud while reading *Amelia and Eleanor Go for a Ride* (Ryan, 1999). Students followed along with their own copies. At one point in the story the reader learns that Eleanor Roosevelt's brother will be *escorting* her to dinner. Susan did a think aloud saying,

> I am not quite sure what *escorting* means in this passage. I did notice the part that follows says Eleanor's husband has to go to a meeting, so I think *escorting*

means her brother will be taking her to dinner rather than her husband because he is very busy with his responsibilities as president.

As Susan and the students read on, the story described the dining table as *elegant*. Again Susan modeled her thinking by saying, "I'm sure eating at the White House would be a very special event, so *elegant* must mean beautiful with everything arranged just perfectly."

Once students gain an understanding of what it means to think aloud, Susan invites them to share their thinking with classmates. However, Susan has found she must provide scaffolding so that students can bring thoughts to a conscious level and then verbally articulate them.

First the class has a discussion about when and how the strategy should be used. Then Susan asks students to underline words or phrases that might have helped her infer the meaning of words and important details for her think alouds. The next step is for students to meet in small groups and practice think aloud techniques. Students are given a copy of "Think Aloud Starters" (see figure 10.1), and Susan models how she would use the prompts. Then students take turns reading aloud and responding to the prompts. While the groups practice think alouds, Susan circulates from group to group and provides feedback.

## Chants

Through Project GLAD training Susan learned to create chants for social studies and science (see figure 10.2). Susan uses a pointer to lead the class in the chant. They discuss vocabulary, and the next time they read the chant they highlight vocabulary words. Students have a stapled booklet of all the chants that are used in the unit. The second time the class sings the chant, students (often ELLs) are picked to place highlight tape over new vocabulary words.

## SUSAN DOWELL'S FAVORITE: "THE FARMER IN THE DELL"

Susan's students love her vocabulary-stretching activity that is based on an idea she learned in her GLAD training. "The Farmer in the Dell" begins with the class generating lists of adjectives, a noun, verbs, adverbs, and prepositional phrases, with each part of speech color coded. Susan records the words and then, using a pointer, guides the class to fill in parts of speech to the tune of "The Farmer in the Dell."(See Figure 10.3) For example, one chart resulted in the following song:

> The brave, adventurous explorer,
> The brave, adventurous explorer,

# Think Aloud Starters

### BEFORE READING

*In this chapter (story or book) I think I might see the vocabulary words_____, _____, and

_____.

(Predicting/Inferring)

### DURING READING

*The word_____makes me see_____,in my mind.
   (Visualizing)
*The word_____ reminds me of _____so it might mean_____.
   (Making Connections)
*I wonder what _____could mean. Because it says _____, it could mean _____.
   (Questioning)

### AFTER READING

*Words that describe this story are _____, _____, and _____.

*My original prediction_____.
   (Checking predictions)
*Traits of the main character     are_____, _____, and _____.
   (Making judgments)

Figure 10.1.   Think Aloud Starters

*Explorer's Rap*
I'm an explorer and I'm here to say,
I love to explore every day!
You can find me sailing the seven seas,
The king and queen I hope to please.

Spices, trade, and gold too!
I'm doing the explorer bugaloo!

I love to explore unknown lands,
Spreading Christianity wherever I can.
Searching for silk and trade routes is my game. I hope it all brings
me wealth and fame.

Spices, trade, and gold too!
I'm doing the explorer bugaloo!
DOING THE EXPLORER BUGALOO!

**Figure 10.2   Vocabulary Chant**

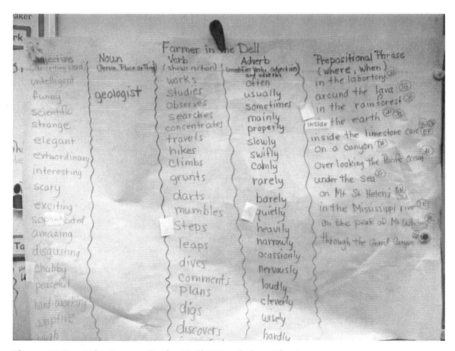

**Figure 10.3.   "The Farmer in the Dell" Vocabulary Chart**

The brave, adventurous explorer
Navigates across the vast ocean.

Next Susan asks individual students to use the pointer and choose which words will make up the song. To extend the activity, she sometimes puts a clean strip of paper over the verbs and changes present tense verbs into past tense or substitutes antonyms for the adjectives.

For another variation of the strategy, Susan creates five sentences from the chart and writes them on sentence strips with the parts of speech color coded. Then the sentences are cut according to color and shuffled. Each group of students receives the same amount of strips. Each group decides what words they want to keep and puts aside the extras to be traded for words they need (e.g., they may have three adverbs, but no adjectives). When the trading is done, each group sings its version of "The Farmer in the Dell."

## CONCLUSION

Susan assesses her students' vocabulary development both formally and informally. When ELLs move up a reading level, Susan knows it can be attributed to their knowledge of vocabulary. Perhaps her greatest thrill comes when she sees students apply what they are learning. Susan shared, "I love it when they are reading silently, yet they are compelled to come up to point out a vocabulary word that we have discussed."

Susan has put a lot of time, commitment, and her own resources into learning as much as she can about how to teach vocabulary. Her students' success is evidence of that!

## REFLECTION AND ACTION

The following questions are designed to help you think through your vocabulary instruction, either alone or with a group of colleagues. The reflection you do is an important part of reading the chapter. The action that results is what puts you among the ranks of great literacy teachers.

1. What is your primary means of professional learning? Is there anything you would like to do to extend that learning?
2. What is the most valuable professional development session you've attended? What made it effective?
3. Develop a vocabulary activity you could use based on a classic children's song. Share it with your colleagues.

4. How many ELLs are in your classroom? What strategies have you tried that were especially effective for them?
5. Much of Susan Dowell's training is based on research indicating that language is acquired most effectively when the emphasis is on meaning. What steps could you take to ensure that vocabulary instruction is embedded into meaningful contexts?
6. What is one thing from this chapter that you would like to include in your own classroom?

## MEETING PROCEDURE: GIVE ONE, GET ONE

| | |
|---|---|
| Purpose: | Participants increase their repertoire of ideas or strategies |
| Advantage: | Everyone contributes |
| | Everyone's ideas are acknowledged and respected |

**Give One**

| | | |
|---|---|---|
| | | |
| | | |

**Get One**

| | | |
|---|---|---|
| | | |
| | | |

Disadvantage:      Ideas that are not best practice might be shared
Steps:

1. Prepare a "give one, get one" page with the number of boxes determined by the concept under discussion.
2. Each person fills in his/her "give one" sections with an idea to address the topic of conversation. For this activity use question 5 from "Reflection and Action."
3. Participants walk around the room and "give one" idea to another person who writes it in one of his/her "get one" spaces. That person then "gives one" to the other person who writes it in his/her "get one" space.

Adapted from Kagan Publishing & Professional Development www.kagan online.com.

## Chapter Eleven

# Vocabulary Instruction for Children with Special Needs

While planning this chapter, I became curious about the origin of the term, *special education*. An initial Google search yielded more than 75 million hits. I did not discover the origin of the phrase, although I thought of many possibilities as I perused some of the sites.

I wish the term *special* had been uttered when the American Association on Mental Deficiency held its first convention in 1947. The term *special* would certainly have been preferable to *deficiency*. The term may have originated in the early 1950s when parent advocates joined forces to establish organizations such as the United Cerebral Palsy Association and the Muscular Dystrophy Association. They understood the *specialness* of their children.

Maybe the term *special education* was first used as John F. Kennedy's Panel on Mental Retardation searched for a more humane way to describe the people for whom they were advocating. Regardless of how and when the exact phrase *special education* was articulated, the word *special* reflects how privileged teachers are to be entrusted with the education of these children.

This chapter is built on the premise that *all children can learn*. However, think about how the meaning of that belief would change if you deleted one little word—*can*. Hopefully when you do, you will realize that learning is not a matter of *can* or *can't*. Simply put, *all children learn*, and learning vocabulary is a key building block for their learning.

### VOCABULARY INSTRUCTION FOR CHILDREN WITH SPECIAL NEEDS IN MAYFIELD, OHIO

For more than thirty years Sally Maher has been teaching children who are hearing impaired. While you may never have a child who is hearing impaired in your classroom, you will certainly have children with disabilities of one kind or another, even if they are only with you for part of the day. What Sally has learned through her years of experience and professional learning is applicable to all children with disabilities because they all struggle with vocabulary at some level.

Sally teaches a kindergarten/first-grade class at Millridge Center for the Hearing Impaired (MCHI) in Mayfield, Ohio. MCHI is a regional program that serves thirty-five school districts. Children with various disabilities enroll at age three. When they become kindergartners they continue at MCHI if their primary disability is a hearing impairment or return to their home schools if not hearing impaired. Some MCHI students have cochlear implants, some wear traditional hearing aids, and some are supported with assistive hearing devices such as sound amplifiers.

MCHI is connected to Millridge Elementary School, so inclusion in mainstream classrooms is part of MCHI's program. Student placement varies depending on the level of need. Children can be fully included with support, included for specific subjects, or placed in a self-contained classroom.

## VOCABULARY ROUTINES

### Scaffolding with Pictures

Sally's students need a great deal of support with visuals when they are learning speaking/listening and reading vocabulary. Often children who are hearing impaired can read common sight words or decode unknown words, but they do not know what the simplest of words mean. Martin was a kindergarten student reading at an early first-grade level. He was able to read 110 out of 150 words on the sight words list. Upon further examination, however, Sally found that Martin could read the words *he* and *she*, but when given pictures he did not know that *he* went with the boy and *she* went with the girl. (Note: All student names are pseudonyms.)

When asked how Martin got that far in reading without understanding the words, Sally explained,

> People assume. When parents help their children at home, they sometimes assume that if the child knows the word, he knows what it means. That's a very bad assumption. I am constantly stopping to ask, "What is that?" or "Do you know what that is?"

Another language barrier many of Sally's students face is that they know an object by its function rather than by its label. For example, when Sally pointed to the sink and asked what it was, Jasmine replied, "That's a wash my hands." When shown a picture of a stove and asked "What is this?" Lillian said, "You cook in it."

Most children hear words repeatedly before they ever begin to speak those words. The repetition allows them to deduce meaning from concrete and verbal clues that are always present when the words are spoken. Children who are hearing impaired typically have missed those clues for the first two years of their lives. "You have to provide a lot of input," Sally remarked. "When students come to us at age three, the primary goal is getting communication in place. They have to have the scaffold of pictures, pictures, pictures!"

## Word Webs

Sally uses word webs as one means for connecting words with pictures. Webs are built around words students will need for state-required science or social studies curricula as well as words students will encounter in literature or nonfiction books they will read as a class. Recently the class was doing a Frank Asch author study. They created a word web for the term *seasons* after they read *Mooncake* (Asch, 2000).

Sally uses the following structured routine for creating word maps:

Day 1: The class creates an illustrated word web based on a key vocabulary term. For the *seasons* map, Sally asked students to provide words for each of the seasons (see figure 11.1). Sally drew a simple picture for each word as she randomly placed the word on the map. Sometimes Sally later adds pictures that she downloads from websites such as Google Images or Boardmaker.

Day 2: The class reviews the words on the map and then puts them into categories. For the *seasons* word map, students named the four seasons and Sally wrote them on the chart. Then students discussed each item and placed it in the appropriate season.

Day 3: The class revisits the word map once more, reading and discussing all the words. Sometimes on this day they will add more words; sometimes they will develop additional categories. For the *seasons* map, for example, the class further divided the items in each season into groups of clothing, sounds, and holidays.

Days 4 and 5: The class revisits the word map and discusses each word. On these days Sally supports language development through conversations about the words, making explicit connections between the words and the curriculum topic or children's book that was the foundation for the map.

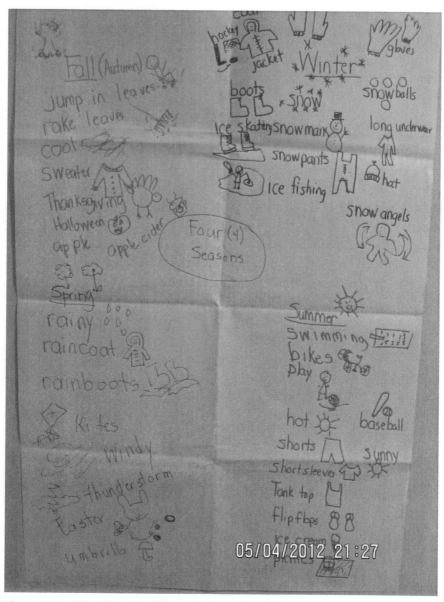

Figure 11.1. Word Map for *Mooncake* by Frank Asch

## Alpha Boxes

For thematic units, Sally's students fill "alpha boxes" with vocabulary words. The activity begins with Sally dividing a piece of chart paper into sections for each letter of the alphabet. As they proceed through the unit, students are encouraged to come up with relevant words that would go into each alpha box. The goal is to get at least one word for each alpha box before the unit is complete (see figure 11.2).

## SALLY MAHER'S FAVORITE: LANGUAGE CALENDAR

Sally's language arts instruction is taken in part from *Phonics in Motion* (Kindervater, 2002). A daily component of the program is the "language calendar," which flows from a hands-on phonics activity the students completed that day. For example, early in the year when the class learned the sound for the letter *p*, Sally read aloud *Harold and the Purple Crayon* (Johnson, 1998). Then over several days, students did various activities with the letter *p*. They wrote their own *p*'s and decorated the page with pink and purple polka dots, pasted pictures on a large *P* (pirate, purse, puppies, pizza, pancakes), and made pink and purple Play-Doh.

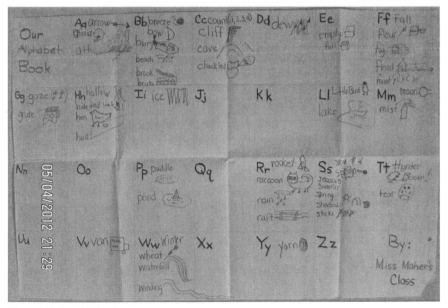

Figure 11.2.  **Alpha Boxes**

After each activity Sally asked students to tell her about what they did as she modeled writing about it on the whiteboard. Teacher and students then read the story aloud together. "My primary purpose is to get language out of them," Sally explained. One copy of the "language calendar" is hung on the wall and stays there for a month. The month's "language calendar" serves as a reference for students' reading and writing (see figure 11.3).

Another copy of the daily language calendar is placed in binders that each child takes home to share with parents. The "language calendar" serves as a daily parent newsletter and also provides the family with a learning activity to do together. Each evening families write about something the child did at home and place the story in the binder. In keeping with Sally's focus on pictures to strengthen vocabulary, parents are encouraged to include an illustration. Sometimes a family member draws an illustration, and sometimes families cut pictures from a variety of print sources such as magazines, cereal box tops, or newspaper ads.

The next day, each child shares his or her story with the class. As the child shares, Sally probes for more language with questions, such as "Tell me what you did" or "How did you feel about what you did?" Students love to look through their binders. "It's like a diary for them," Sally claimed. "If for some reason I don't do it, they sulk."

**Figure 11.3.   Language Calendar**

## CONCLUSION

In chapter 1 you read about how low vocabulary acquisition cuts across socioeconomic status and about the importance of classroom discussions. Although Sally's students have needs that are unique to children who have a hearing impairment, her instructional strategies can be used with any child who has a vocabulary deficit. Sally's focus on using pictures to illustrate words will provide a scaffold for any child who needs extra support in building vocabulary. It's not just the special education students who need this support. Any child who struggles is *special*!

## REFLECTION AND ACTION

The following questions are designed to help you think through your vocabulary instruction, either alone or with a group of colleagues. The reflection you do is an important part of reading the chapter. The action that results is what puts you among the ranks of great literacy teachers.

1. Reflect on the revised mantra: *All children learn.* How does it challenge teachers to think differently about student learning?
2. Have you had children with a hearing impairment in your classroom? If so, describe how you made accommodations for that child. If not, what would be the first thing you would want to know if a child with a hearing impairment were mainstreamed into your classroom?
3. Research the differences between programs that use American Sign Language and programs that are auditory-verbal. Share what you learned with your colleagues. (Note: MCHI's program is auditory-verbal.)
4. How are children with hearing disabilities served in your area? Interview a teacher of hearing-impaired students. What did the teacher share that is similar to Sally Maher's beliefs and instruction? What is different?
5. What is your biggest challenge with meeting the needs of mainstreamed children? With your discussion group, respond to this question using the meeting procedure, "kiva," below.
6. What is one thing from this chapter that you would like to include in your own classroom?

## MEETING PROCEDURE: KIVA

Purpose: To allow participants to consider an important issue from different perspectives

Advantages:            Generates reflective conversation
                       Works well for large groups
Disadvantage:          Some participants may be intimidated when being ob-
                       served
Steps:

1. Participants are seated in tiered circles.
2. The inner tier responds initially to a question posed and has approximately
   fifteen minutes to discuss. For this activity use question 5 from "Reflection and Action."
3. The outer tiers listen and take notes.
4. At the end of fifteen minutes, the inner tier moves to the outer tier. The
   new inner tier responds to the same question and can respond to comments
   made by the initial inner tier.
5. The exchange continues until each tier has participated. If time permits,
   the process can be repeated. The dialogue will change depending on previously made comments.

## Chapter Twelve

# Oral Vocabulary
# Leads Reading Vocabulary

In chapter 1 you read about the *30 million-word gap*, results of a study that found by age four, children of professional families heard 45 million words, whereas children of mothers who were on welfare heard only 13 million words (Hart & Risley, 2003). The follow-up study showed the 30 million-word gap was a strong predictor of third-grade reading comprehension. Another study by Cunningham and Stanovich (1997) found that vocabulary size in first grade strongly predicted reading comprehension in eleventh grade—ten years later!

Listening vocabulary runs ahead of reading vocabulary and pulls it along. Decoding and sight word recognition is futile if the words are not in the student's listening vocabulary. We dare not underestimate the importance of helping students of all ages develop their listening (receptive) vocabularies.

## ORAL LANGUAGE INSTRUCTION
## IN SPRINGFIELD, MISSOURI

Abby Lowe walks a fine line between underestimating and overestimating what her students know and can do. "My students are young, and some are English language learners," she explained. "I can't assume they know the language I am using. I have to think it through. If I tell them to put the crayons in the tub, I have to assume some might not know what a tub is." The paradox is that Abby also believes we often underestimate the vocabulary of young students and ELLs. "We think they can't understand big words," she stated. "If I expect it, they will learn it."

Abby teaches all-day kindergarten at David Harrison Elementary School in Springfield, Missouri, a large district with a diverse population. She is released from her classroom every Wednesday morning so that she can serve the other K–2 teachers and students in her assignment as literacy leader. One-third of the students in Abby's school receive free or reduced cost lunches, but there are also large numbers of children from middle- and upper-class homes. About 15 percent of the students are English language learners (ELLs). Some of the ELLs are Hispanic; large numbers of ELLs are of Russian, Chinese, or Vietnamese heritage. Many speak no English when they enter kindergarten.

Abby's students reflect the makeup of the school as a whole. She describes their backgrounds as "very diverse." She explained,

> Many of my students have no preschool, no trips to the zoo, no books in their homes. Others have been read to since they were in the womb, attended quality preschools, and are already reading when they start kindergarten. The diversity presents a challenge.

## VOCABULARY ROUTINES

Since Abby teaches five-year-olds, her focus is on indirect instruction for listening and speaking vocabulary. She is adamant, however, that oral vocabulary acquisition is "very, very important" in upper grades as well. Here are some of the ways Abby helps her students learn new words.

### Structured Conversations

Abby provides many opportunities for students to talk with one another throughout the school day. "Because the population is diverse, they can learn so much from one another," she believes. However, Abby doesn't leave anything to chance. In addition to informal talking time, Abby plans times when conversations are structured.

Early in the year Abby and her students together generate rules for classroom conversation—what it sounds like (speaking) and what it looks like (listening) (see figure 12.1). Although many students can't read the posted rules, Abby displays these "anchor charts" on the wall for those who can read them and as a concrete reminder even for those who can't. The class continually revisits the rules and adds to them as their conversations become lengthier and the students mature in their listening and speaking.

What do students talk about in these structured conversations? "Everything, everything, everything," Abby says.

> Sometimes I ask them to make text-to-self connections related to read alouds. Sometimes they make predictions. Sometimes they talk about what they will

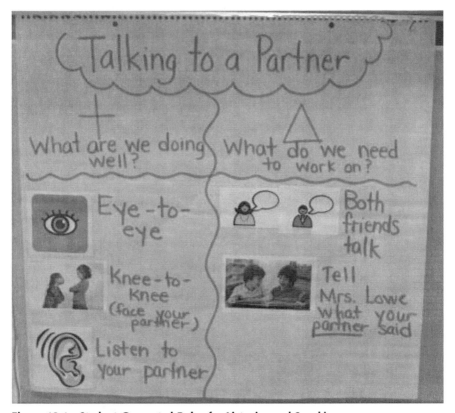

**Figure 12.1   Student-Generated Rules for Listening and Speaking**

write during writer's workshop. Sometimes I just let them talk about what they did on the weekend. I nearly always tell them what I want them to talk about so that they learn to stay on topic.

Whom do students talk with? Sometimes students "turn and talk" with someone they are near. More often Abby is intentional about how she pairs students. She likes to pair ELLs with students who will be good language role models. How often do they turn and talk? Abby simply replied, "A lot! They have several opportunities every day." Initially Abby keeps the conversations short. She listens to hear that students are staying on track. If they start to digress, or if there is a lull in the noise level, she knows it is time to move on.

Often the partner conversations are based on a cooperative learning strategy called "think-pair-share." (See Figure 12.2) Abby poses a question, problem, or other prompt. She instructs everyone to "think." After a reasonable wait time, she then tells the students to "pair." At that point they tell their partners what they were thinking. Finally, when Abby says, "share," students

**Figure 12.2.   Student-Illustrated Think-Pair-Share Chart**

raise their hands to share with the class the conversation they had with their partners.

## Teacher Modeling

Abby makes sure to structure her own use of words, too. She consciously thinks of words she can use in her ongoing interaction with students to develop their vocabulary. For example, she uses synonyms for common terms like *on*, *under*, and *behind*. She will say, "It's just below the light," rather than, "It's under the light." After hearing the synonyms several times, students begin using them as well. Abby finds that structured conversations "just naturally" result in an increase in vocabulary.

## Informal Social Language Development

Many of Abby's students don't know how to use social vocabulary like *please*, *thank you*, *may I*, *can you*, and so on. Rather than requesting help, students will sometimes reach out and grab an object. Abby models "how we talk to friends when we need something." Usually she then asks a few students to act it out for the rest of the class.

For example, when students are sharing supplies, a student might reach across the table to grab a pair of scissors. When she sees this, Abby uses it as a teachable moment with a small group of students, or sometimes with the whole class if appropriate. She might say, "I noticed you reached across to get the scissors. But I see that Amaya is right by the scissors. How could we use our words to ask Amaya to help? Sometimes I hear friends say, 'Amaya, can you please hand me the scissors?' You try it!" Abby then asks a child to repeat the request while the rest of the group listens. Abby continues to model how Amaya can use words to respond appropriately by instructing, "Amaya, now what could you say? How about, 'Here are the scissors, Jacob.'"

## Parent Newsletters

Abby's weekly parent newsletter includes new words the class will be talking about that week. (See Figure 12.3) Abby shared, "At first some parents call and ask, 'Are they going to be tested on these words?' I encourage parents to reinforce the words at home, and they usually do." In addition parents will comment on words their children have learned through read alouds and structured conversations. "He said the word *gumption*. He said I had a lot of *gumption*," one parent laughed. "How did he learn the word *gumption*?"

## ABBY LOWE'S FAVORITE: KINESTHETIC READ ALOUDS

Research has consistently found that read alouds result in vocabulary development when adults intentionally talk about new words encountered in the reading (Justice, 2002; Walsh & Blewitt, 2006). Abby's read aloud sessions are well planned. She looks through her read aloud selections beforehand and targets vocabulary words to teach. After she reads the book aloud, she

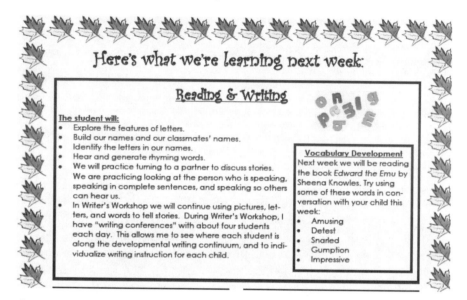

**Figure 12.3. Parent Newsletter Excerpt**

guides the students through a discussion about the words she has chosen using the structured conversation procedures above. Then she gets the students involved in a kinesthetic activity, such as drawing or acting to strengthen the words in their memories.

Recently as Abby read aloud *Edward the Emu* (Knowles & Clement, 1998), students encountered the word *amusing*. Abby read aloud, "The seals are always amusing, it's true, but the lion's the best thing to see at the zoo." The story did not explicitly define the word *amusing*, so Abby and the students talked about what the word means, their own experiences with the word, and what the seals might have done that was amusing. Abby gave several examples and asked students to give a thumbs-up if that situation would be *amusing*, and a thumbs-down if it would not be *amusing*. She asked the students, "Is a clown amusing? Yes, of course! Clowns make me laugh! What about when a friend falls down and scrapes their knee? Is that amusing? No, that's not amusing."

Abby then asked students to turn to their partners and tell them something they think is amusing. Joey told an elaborate story about a time when his dog was chasing a squirrel. He said, "We were laughing so much! It was so amusing!" Abby then asked students to act out how they would feel if they saw something amusing: "What would your face look like? Your body?"

Another time the class came upon the word *revolting* in the book *Gregory, the Terrible Eater* (Sharmat, 2009). In this story, Gregory the goat refuses to eat garbage like the rest of the goats and instead prefers to eat fruits, vegetables, and other healthy foods. In response to Gregory's eating habits, his father says, "It's revolting." The following conversation ensued.

Abby began by asking students what they thought Gregory's father meant. "Do you think Gregory's father likes the foods Gregory eats?" Gaige responded, "No! He wants him to eat trash like they do!" Abby responded, "I think you're right. Mother Goat and Father Goat look disappointed in the illustration, don't they? Father Goat said he thinks the foods Gregory likes are revolting. What do you think that means?" "I think it means it's gross!" said Danielle. Abby responded,

> You're really thinking about what's happening in the story, Danielle! You're right. *Revolting* means really gross, like it makes you feel almost sick to your tummy. Gregory's parents think healthy foods are revolting; they think they're really gross. But I like fruits and vegetables. Different things are revolting to different people. I think asparagus is revolting. I don't like how it tastes at all. What do you think is revolting?

A few students raised their hands and responded in complete sentences, using the vocabulary word. "I think broccoli is revolting . . . Yuck!" said Jarrett. "One time I ate this fish my mom made, and I almost threw up. I held my nose and ate it. It was revolting," said Will.

Abby continued the conversation: "Friends, I want you to think about something you think is revolting. When you turn to your partner, make sure you tell them in a complete sentence what you think is revolting." Students then talked with their partners. Abby concluded the conversation by saying, "I noticed when you were talking to your partners about things you think are revolting, you were all making faces. Show me what your face looks like when you think about something that's revolting!" Students acted out what revolting looks like. Students were then asked to draw a picture of something that's revolting.

The important point to these examples is that Abby doesn't just leave vocabulary acquisition to chance when she reads aloud. She carefully structures conversations so that her students move along the word knowledge continuum.

## CONCLUSION

Abby advises that teachers, "let kids drive vocabulary instruction. If they are interested in a particular subject, then work with vocabulary related to that subject. Sometimes they will just say, 'What does that mean?'" Most importantly, Abby concluded,

> Sometimes teachers and parents assume students don't know the big words, and it's true, we shouldn't assume that they do. But don't dumb down your language with children. Use vocabulary-building words, and then work to help them understand what the words mean.

## REFLECTION AND ACTION

The following questions are designed to help you think through your vocabulary instruction, either alone or with a group of colleagues. The reflection you do is an important part of reading the chapter. The action that results is what puts you among the ranks of great literacy teachers.

1. Think about the fine line between overestimating and underestimating children's potential, which Abby described in the first paragraph. Does this fine line apply to your students? How can you deal with this in your own classroom?
2. To what extent do you peruse your read alouds beforehand to determine vocabulary words you would like to teach? Is this something you could do more often?
3. Many teachers ask their students to "turn and talk" to the person next to them. Is this a routine you use? How could you add more structure to "turn and talk"?
4. Abby is adamant that older students need time in school to develop their listening and speaking vocabularies. Do you agree? To what extent do you think that happens? What is your evidence? Use the "silent Conversations" strategy below with your discussion group to explore this issue.
5. What is one thing from this chapter that you would like to include in your own classroom?

## MEETING PROCEDURE: SILENT CONVERSATION

| | |
|---|---|
| Purpose: | To provide a means for people to express opinions |
| Advantage: | All voices are heard |
| | It is "safe" because it is anonymous |
| | Opinions can be challenged without worry about hurt feelings |
| Disadvantage: | Difficult to do with large groups |

Responses sometimes tend to be surface level rather than thought provoking (I agree, nice job, etc.)

Steps:

1. Pose the issue to be discussed (question 4 in "Reflection and Action").
2. At the beginning of the meeting ask each person to respond in writing on a letter-size piece of paper—NO NAMES.
3. Each person throws his/her paper into the center of the table; then each person picks one up.
4. Read what you picked up, write a response, question, comment, and throw it back into the center.
5. Pick up another. Read what everyone else wrote and respond again.
6. Repeat the process until everyone has seen most papers.
7. Find your own paper and read and reflect on what others had to say.
8. Comment to the group on something interesting you read on a paper other than your own.

# Chapter Thirteen

# Resources

## ONLINE RESOURCES

### Online Dictionaries

*A.Word.A.Day*

http://www.wordsmith.org/awad/ Have a new word come straight into your e-mail every day! The site provides a vocabulary word, its definition, pronunciation information with audio clip, etymology, usage example, and quotation.

*Allwords.com*

http://www.allwords.com/ This online dictionary does a multilingual search that ELL students will find useful. "Links for Word Lovers" will take you to various resources for information (dictionaries, thesaurus, etymologies) and wordplay (puns, rhymes, songs, quotations).

*AskOxford.com*

http://www.askoxford.com/ This online dictionary includes word games and other support materials for spelling, grammar, etymology, and foreign phrases, plus an "Ask the Experts" link where you can find answers to frequently asked questions about language.

*Merriam Webster*

http://www.merriam-webster.com/quiz/index.htm At this website you can take a ten-question quiz to determine how strong your vocabulary is. There are dozens of different versions so you can try it as often as you like.

*Vocabulary*
http://www.vocabulary.com/ Vocabulary makes the words on any web page into links so that you can look them up with just a click.

*Word Central*
http://www.wordcentral.com This website allows students to build their own dictionaries.

## Websites for Professional Reading

*Reading Online*
http://www.readingonline.org/articles/art_index.asp?HREF=/articles/curtis /index.html *Teaching Vocabulary to Adolescents to Improve Comprehension.* This article addresses vocabulary learning, moving from isolation to context, and selecting words for instruction.

*Reading Rockets*
http://www.readingrockets.org/article/21160 *Instruction of Metacognitive Strategies Enhances Reading Comprehension and Vocabulary Achievement of Third-Grade Students.* This article addresses the vocabulary-comprehension connection.

## Websites with Instructional Strategies

*Choice Literacy*
http://www.choiceliteracy.com/public/416.cfm At this website Franki Sibberson shares some of her favorite children's literature for word work.

*Ed Helper*
http://edhelper.com/vocabulary_board_game.htm At this site you will find instructions and a template for creating your own vocabulary board games.

*Just Read Now*
http://www.justreadnow.com/strategies/vocabulary.htm *Just Read Now: Vocabulary Strategies.* This page includes twelve different vocabulary strategies for the middle school.

*Manatee County Schools: Vocabulary Builders (Grades 3–5)*
http://www.manatee.k12.fl.us/sites/elementary/samoset/resources/rvocab index.htm This website offers activities on prefixes, suffixes, antonyms, synonyms, homophones, multiple meanings, context, and more. Students will find the online student dictionary useful.

*Prince George's County Public Schools: Teaching Vocabulary in the Content Areas*
http://www.pgcps.pg.k12.md.us/%7Eelc/readingacross2.html This page contains specific tips for teaching content reading vocabulary words, prefixes, suffixes, etc.

*Reading Resource*
http://www.readingresource.net/vocabularyactivities.html This website offers free reprintable downloads and resources that have been reviewed and endorsed by teachers.

*San Diego State University: Reading in the Content Areas: Study Guides and Vocabulary Activities*
http://coe.sdsu.edu/people/jmora/Pages/ContentStudyGds.htm This page includes activities for teaching vocabulary in content areas.

*THE PRACTICE: Vocabulary Development*
http://knowledgeloom.org/practice_basedoc.jsp?t=1&bpid=1207&aspect=1 &location=2&parentid=1197&bpinterid=1197&spotlightid=1174&testflag= yes This site provides an overview of vocabulary development in content areas. It includes links to other sites.

*Vocabulary University*
http://www.vocabulary.com/ This website has numerous lesson plans, word puzzles, and activities.

*Wordle*
http://www.wordle.net/ At this website, students can generate "word clouds" for their vocabulary words. Clouds can be customized with different fonts, layouts, and color schemes.

## Websites for Teaching Word Roots

*Dictionary*
http://dictionary.reference.com/browse/root+word This comprehensive dictionary provides the meanings of Greek and Latin roots.

*Fact Monster*
http://www.factmonster.com/ipka/A0907017.html Fact Monster offers information and activities based on Latin and Greek roots.

*Learn that Word*
http://www.learnthat.org/pages/view/roots.html This site claims the most complete root word list and suffix list on the Web.

*Robertson's Words for a Modern Age*
http://www.wordinfo.info/ Here you will find a dictionary of Latin and Greek words used in modern English vocabulary.

*Word Explorations*
http://www.wordexplorations.com/ This website includes many references and interesting resources. Students will enjoy "Words for Our Modern Age: Especially English Words from Greek and Latin Sources."

## PROFESSIONAL BOOKS

Allen, J. (1999). *Words, words, words: Teaching vocabulary in grades 4–12.* Portland, ME: Stenhouse.

Baer, D., Invernizzi, M., Templeton, S., & Johnston, F. (2007). *Words their way: Word study for phonics, vocabulary, and spelling instruction.* New York: Prentice Hall.

Beck, I., McKeown, M., & Kucan, L. (2002). *Bringing words to life: Robust vocabulary instruction.* New York: Guilford Press.

Johnston, F., Invernizzi, M., & Bear, D. R. (2004). *Words their way: Word sorts for syllables and affixes spellers.* New York: Prentice Hall.

Marzano, R. J., & Pickering, D. J. (2005). *Building academic vocabulary: Teachers manual.* Alexandria, VA: Association of Supervision and Curriculum Development.

Newton, E., Padak, N. D., & Timothy, T. V. (2008). *Evidence-based instruction in reading: A professional development guide to vocabulary.* Boston: Pearson.

Rasinski, T. (2005). *Daily word ladders: Grades 2–3.* New York: Teaching Resources.

Rasinski, T. (2005). *Daily word ladders: Grades 4–6.* New York: Teaching Resources.

Rasinski, T., & Brothers, K. (2006). *Poems for word study, grades K–1.* Huntington Beach, CA: Shell Educational Publishing.

Rasinski, T., & Brothers, K. (2006). *Poems for word study, grades 1–2.* Huntington Beach, CA: Shell Educational Publishing.

Rasinski, T., & Brothers, K. (2006). *Poems for word study, grades 2–3.* Huntington Beach, CA: Shell Educational Publishing.

Rasinski, T., & Heym, R. (2006). *Making & writing words: 41 sequenced word-building lessons.* Huntington Beach, CA: Shell Educational Publishing.

Rasinski, T. V., Padak, N. D., Church, B., Fawcett, G., Hendershot, J., Henry, J. M., Peck, J. K., Pryor, E., & Roskos, K. (Eds.). (2000). *Teaching word recognition, spelling, and vocabulary: Strategies from* The Reading Teacher. Newark, DE: International Reading Association.

Rasinski, T., Padak, N., Newton, R. M., & Newton, E. (2008). *Greek & Latin roots: Keys to building vocabulary.* Huntington Beach, CA: Shell Educational Publishing.

## CHILDREN'S LITERATURE FOR TEACHING VOCABULARY

Alda. A. (2011). *Did you say pears?* Plattsburg, NY: Tundra Books.

Brisson, P. (2004). *Beach is to fun.* New York: Henry Holt.

Cleary, B. P. (2001). *Hairy, scary, ordinary: What is an adjective?* Minneapolis: Learners Publishing Group.

Cleary, B. P. (2007). *How much can a bare bear bear? What are homonyms and homophones?* Minneapolis: First Avenue Editions.

Frasier, D. (2007). *Miss Alenius: A vocabulary disaster.* Mooloolaba, Queensland, Australia: Sandpiper.

Gwynne, F. (1988). *A chocolate mousse for dinner.* New York: Aladdin.

Gwynne, F. (1988). *The king who rained.* New York: Aladdin.

O'Connor, J. (2005). *Fancy Nancy.* New York: HarperCollins.

O'Connor, J. (2007). *Fancy Nancy and the posh puppy.* New York: HarperCollins.

O'Connor, J. (2008). *Fancy Nancy: Bonjour, butterfly.* New York: HarperCollins.

O'Connor, J. (2008). *Fancy Nancy's favorite fancy words: From accessories to zany.* New York: HarperCollins.

Piven, H. (2007). *My dog is as smelly as dirty socks: And other funny family portraits.* New York: Schwartz & Wade. .

Ross, A., & Gwynne, F. (1998). *A little pigeon toad.* New York: Aladdin.

Scanlon, E. (2004). *A sock is a pocket for your toes: A pocket book.* New York: HarperCollins.

Terban, M. (2008). *Eight ate: A feast of homonym riddles.* Mooloolaba, Queensland, Australia: Sandpiper.

Tobias, T. (1998). *A world of words: An ABC of quotations.* New York: Lothrop Lee & Shepard.

Tobias, T. (2000). *Serendipity.* New York: Simon & Schuster.

Ziefert, H., & Rap, J. (2005). *Misery is a smell in your backpack.* Maplewood, NJ: Blue Apple..

# References

## REFERENCES

Allen, J. (1999). *Words, words, words: Teaching vocabulary in grades 4–12.* Portland, ME: Stenhouse.

Allington, R. L. (1977). If they don't read much, how they ever gonna get good? *Journal of Reading* 21, 57–61.

Barth, R. S. (2001). *Learning by heart.* San Francisco: Jossey-Bass.

Baumann, J. F., Kame'enui, E. J., & Ask, G. E. (2003). Research on vocabulary instruction: Voltaire redux. In J. Flood, D. Lapp, J. R. Squire ,& J. M. Jensen (Eds.), *Handbook of research on teaching the English language arts* (2nd ed.), 752–85. Mahwah, NJ: Lawrence Erlbaum Associates.

Bear, D. R., Invernizzi, M., Templeton, S., & Johnston, F. (2008). *Words their way: Word study for phonics, vocabulary, and spelling instruction.* Upper Saddle River, NJ: Pearson.

Beck, I. L., McKeown, M. G., & Kucan, L. (2002). *Bringing words to life: Robust vocabulary instruction.* New York: Guilford Press.

Biemiller, A. (2001). Teaching vocabulary: Early, direct, and sequential. *American Educator, 25* (1), 24–28.

Blachowicz, C. L. Z., & Fisher, P. (2000). Vocabulary instruction. In M. L. Kamil, P. B. Mosenthal, P. D. Pearson & R. Barr (Eds.), *Handbook of reading research: Volume 3*, 503–23. Mahwah, NJ: Lawrence Erlbaum Associates.

Block, C. ,& Mangieri, J. (2002). Recreational reading: Twenty years later. *The Reading Teacher* 58, 154–67.

Chall, J. S., Curtis, J. S., Curtis, M. E., & Kearns, G. (2005). *Diagnostic assessment: Reading grades 1–6* (2nd ed.). Orlando, FL: Houghton Mifflin.

Chall, J. S., & Jacobs, V. A. (2003, Spring). Research roundup: Poor children's fourth-grade slump. *American Educator.* Retrieved July 15, 2010, from http://www.aft.org/newspubs/periodicals/ae/spring2003/hirschbclassic.cfm.

Cohen, K. (1999). Reluctant eighth grade readers enjoy sustained silent reading. *California Reader* 33 (1), 22–25.

Cunningham, A. E., & Stanovich, K. (1997). Early reading acquisition and its relation to reading experience and ability 10 years later. *Developmental Psychology* 33 (6), 934–45.

Curtis, M. E,. & Longo, A. M. (2001). Teaching vocabulary to adolescents to improve comprehension. *Reading Online* 5 (4). Retrieved July 15, 2010, from http://www.readingonline.org/articles/curtis/.

Dale, E. (1965). Vocabulary measurement: Techniques and major findings. *Elementary English* 42, 895–901, 948.

Fiderer, A. (1995). *Practical assessments for literature-based reading classrooms.* New York: Scholastic.

Forget, M. A. (2004). *MAX teaching with reading and writing: Classroom activities for helping students learn new subject matter while acquiring literacy skills.* Victoria, BC, Canada: Trafford.

Good, R. H., & Kaminski, R. (2001). *Dynamic indicators of basic early literacy skills.* Eugene: University of Oregon Center on Teaching and Learning.

Hajdusiewicz, B. B. (1999). *More phonics through poetry: Teaching phonemic awareness using poetry, grades 2–3.* Glenview, IL: Good Year Books.

Hansen, J. (2010). Teaching without talking. *Phi Delta Kappan* 91 (1), 35–40.

Hart, B. & Risley, T. R. (2003, Spring). The early catastrophe: The 30 million word gap by age 3. *American Educator.* Retrieved on July 5, 2010, from http://www.aft.org/newspubs/periodicals/ae/spring2003/index.cfm.

Herda, R., & Ramos, F. (2001). How consistently do students read during sustained silent reading? *California School Library Journal* 24 (2), 29–31.

How many repetitions does the human brain need to learn words for good? (2010). Retrieved July 15, 2010, from http://pidict.com/learning/repetitions.html.

Justice, L. M. (2002). Word exposure conditions and preschoolers' novel word learning during shared storybook reading. *Reading Psychology* 23 (2), 87–106.

Kindervater, T. (2002). *Phonics in motion.* Gates Mills, OH: Author.

Krashen, S. (2001). More smoke and mirrors: A critique of the National Reading Panel report on fluency. *Phi Delta Kappan* 83, 119–23.

Krashen, S. (2004, April). *Free voluntary reading: New research, applications, and controversies.* Paper presented at the meeting of Regional Language Center, Singapore.

Marzano, R. J. (2004). *Classroom instruction that works: Research-based strategies for increasing student achievement.* Upper Saddle River, NJ: Prentice Hall.

McGinley, W. J., & Denner, P. R. (1987). Story impressions: A pre-reading/writing activity. *Journal of Reading* 31, 248–53.

McKenna, M. C., & Stahl, S. A. (2003). *Assessment for reading instruction.* New York: Guilford Press.

McKeown, M. G., Beck, I. L., Omanson, R. C., & Pople, M. T. (1985). Some effects of the nature and frequency of vocabulary instruction on the knowledge of use of words. *Reading Research Quarterly* 20, 522–35.

Measures of Academic Performance. Lake Oswego, OR: Northwest Evaluation Association. Available online: www.nwea.org.

Morrow, L. M., & Tracey, D. H. (2007). Best practices in early literacy development in preschool, kindergarten, and first grade. In L. B. Gambrell, L. M. Morrow & M. Pressley (Eds.), *Best practices in literacy education* (3rd ed.), 57–82. New York: Guilford Press.

Nagy, W. E. (1988). *Teaching vocabulary to improve reading comprehension.* Newark, DE: International Reading Association.

Nagy, W. E., & Anderson, R. C. (1984). How many words are there in printed school English? *Reading Research Quarterly* 19, 304–30.

Nagy, W. E., Anderson, R. C., & Herman, R. (1987). Learning word meanings from context during normal reading. *American Educational Research Journal* 24, 237–70.

National Reading Panel. (2000). *Report of the National Reading Panel: Teaching children to read. Report of the subgroups.* Washington, DC: U.S. Department of Health and Human Services, National Institute of Health.

Padak, N., & Rasinski, T. (2005). *Fast Start for early readers: A research-based, send-home literacy program with 60 reproducible poems and activities that ensures reading success for every child.* New York: Scholastic.

Pearson, P. D. ,& Gallagher, M. C. (1983). The instruction of reading comprehension. *Contemporary Educational Psychology* 8, 317–44.

Rasinski, T. V. (2003). *The fluent reader.* New York: Scholastic.

Rasinski, T. V. (2008). *Daily word ladders: Grades 1–2: 150+ reproducible word study lessons that help kids boost reading, vocabulary, spelling and phonics skills!* New York: Scholastic.

Rasinski, T., Padak, N., & Fawcett, G. (2010). *Teaching children who find reading difficult* (4th ed.). Boston, MA: Pearson.

Rasinski, T , Padak, N., Newton, R. M., & Newton, E. (2007). *Building vocabulary from word roots.* Huntington Beach, CA: Beach City Press.

Rasinksi, T. V., Padak, N. D., Newton, R. N. ,& Newton, E. (2008). *Greek and Latin roots: Keys to building vocabulary.* Huntington Beach, CA: Shell Educational Publishing.

Reading Research (2009–2010). Retrieved July 15, 2010, from http://www .summitcharter.org/Reading_Research.

Reeves, D. B. (2000). *Accountability in action: A blueprint for learning organizations.* Denver: Advanced Learning Press.

Rosen, L. (2010). *Rewired: Understanding the iGeneration and the way they learn.* New York: Palgrave Macmillan.

Rowe, M. B. (1972). *Wait-time and rewards as instructional variables, their influence in language, logic, and fate control.* Paper presented at the National Association for Research in Science Teaching, Chicago.

Sanders, W. & Rivers, J.C., (1996). *Cumulative and residual effects of teachers on students' future achievement.* Knoxville: University of Tennessee Value-Added Research Center.

Smith, F. (1987). *Joining the literacy club: Further essays into education.* Portsmouth, NH: Heinemann.

Stahl, S. A. (1998). Four questions about vocabulary knowledge and reading and some answers. In C. Hynd (Ed.), *Learning from text across conceptual domains,* 15–44. Mahwah, NJ: Lawrence Erlbaum.

Stahl, S. A. (2003a). Vocabulary and readability: How knowing word meanings affects comprehension. *Topics in Language Disorders* 23 (3), 241–48.

Stahl, S. A. (2003b, Spring). How words are learned incrementally over time. *American Educator,* 18–19, 44.

Stahl, S. A., & Fairbanks, M. M. (1986). The effects of vocabulary instruction: A model-based meta-analysis. *Review of Educational Research* 56 (1), 72–110.

Stanovich, K. E. (1986). Matthew effects in reading: Some consequences of individual differences in the acquisition of literacy. *Reading Research Quarterly* 21, 360–407.

Vecchio, A. (Executive Producer). (2010, July 13). WKYC Channel 3 News. Cleveland, OH: WKYC.

Von Sprecken, D., & Krashen, S. (1998). Do students read during sustained silent reading? *California Reader* 32 (1), 11–13.

Walsh, B. A., & Blewitt, P. (2006). The effect of questioning style during storybook reading on novel vocabulary acquisition of preschoolers. *Early Childhood Education Journal* 33 (4),. 273–78.

## LITERATURE CITED

Asch, F. (2000). *Mooncake.* New York: Aladdin.

Barrett, J., & Barrett, R. (1978). *Cloudy with a chance of meatballs.* New York: Atheneum.

Carle, E. (1987). *The very hungry caterpillar.* New York: Philomel.

Dahl, R. (1988). *Matilda.* New York: Penguin.

DiCamillo, K. (2009). *Because of Winn-Dixie.* Somerville, MA: Candlewick.

DiCamillo, K. ,& VanDusen, C. (2009). *Mercy Watson goes for a ride.* Somerville, MA: Candlewick.

Dostoyevsky, F. (1989). *Crime and punishment (*3rd ed). New York: W. W. Norton.

Estes, E. (1994). *The hundred dresses.* Orlando, FL: Harcourt.

Janzen, R. (2010). *Mennonite in a little black dress: A memoir of going home.* New York: Henry Holt.

Johnson, C. (1998). *Harold and the purple crayon.* New York: HarperCollins.

Knowles, S., & Clement, R. (1998). *Edward the emu.* New York: HarperCollins.

Lowry, L. (2003). *The giver.* Orlando, FL: Houghton Mifflin.

Mosel, A. (adapted). (2007). *Tiki Tiki Tembo.* New York: Square Fish.

O'Dell, S. (1987). *Island of the blue dolphins.* New York: Dell.

Park, L. S. (2003). *A single shard.* New York: Yearling.

Pitts, P. (1988). *Racing the sun.* New York: HarperCollins.

Ryan, P. M. (1999). *Amelia and Eleanor go for a ride.* New York: Scholastic.

Sharmat, M. (2009). *Gregory the terrible eater.* New York: Scholastic.

Steig. W. (2011). *The amazing bone.* New York: Square Fish.

Steptoe, J. (1987). *Mufaro's beautiful daughters.* New York: Lothrop, Lee & Shepard.

White, E. B. (2001). *Charlotte's web.* New York: HarperCollins.

Wood. A. (1991). *The napping house.* Orlando, FL: Harcourt.

# About the Author

**Gay Fawcett** has been in education for over thirty-eight years as a teacher, principal, language arts consultant, and curriculum director. She also directed Kent State University's Research Center for Educational Technology. She currently teaches online and face-to-face courses for several universities and provides curriculum consultation for schools and school districts. She has authored and/or coauthored more than ninety articles, books, and book chapters for educational publications including the *Phi Delta Kappan*, *Educational Leadership*, *Language Arts*, *The Reading Teacher*, and others. She served as an associate editor of *The Reading Teacher* for six years. Dr. Fawcett earned a bachelor's degree in elementary education and a master's degree in reading from the University of Akron. She was awarded a Ph.D. in curriculum and instruction with an emphasis in literacy from Kent State University. Her dissertation received three awards, including ASCD's Outstanding Dissertation Award.